Sinners AND Saints

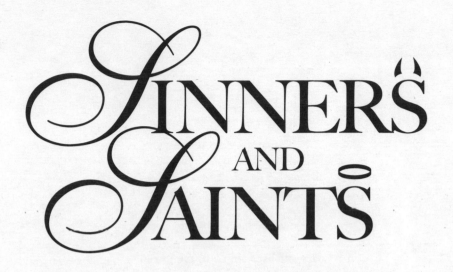

SINNERS
AND
SAINTS

Father MICHAEL SEED
with Noel Botham

metro

Published by Metro Publishing
an imprint of John Blake Publishing Ltd
3 Bramber Court, 2 Bramber Road,
London W14 9PB, England

www.johnblakepublishing.co.uk

First published in hardback in 2009

ISBN: 978 1 84454 770 8

British Library Cataloguing-in-Publication Data:

A catalogue record for this book is available from the British Library.

Design by www.envydesign.co.uk

Printed in the UK by CPI William Clowes Beccles NR34 7TL

1 3 5 7 9 10 8 6 4 2

Papers used by John Blake Publishing are natural, recyclable products made
from wood grown in sustainable forests. The manufacturing processes conform
to the environmental regulations of the country of origin.

Every attempt has been made to contact the relevant copyright-holders,
but some were unsuccessful. We would be happy to rectify the appropriate
acknowledgements in future editions.

This book is dedicated to the life and memory of Cardinal Basil Hume OSB OM and The Rt Hon Alan Clark MP in this tenth year of their joining the hosts of sinners and saints eternally Thursday June 17th and Sunday September 5th 1999

CONTENTS

$\mathscr{I}$NTRODUCTION

I have been blessed in my adult life with a life full of fun and with a great many friends, in the main far more infamous than myself, with whom to share the joy and the laughter. Even the sad times – and there have been, thankfully, few in my adult life – have been made more bearable by the comfort and understanding of those same friends.

As Ecumenical Advisor to two Cardinals at Westminster Cathedral, and honorary priest to the Commons and the Lords, for more than twenty years, I enjoyed a unique and privileged position from which to observe and participate in fascinating national and world events as they unfolded. And I discovered that behind the serious faces which our governors and leaders present to the public, there is, quite often concealed, a far more irreverent and comical side, which I believe (if known) would make them a great deal more human and appealing.

Like my late good friend Alan Clark, I have always kept a diary of sorts and have now decided to reveal some of my favourite treasures contained therein, sharing some anecdotes about the generally friendly – and some not so friendly – people I have encountered along the way. Hopefully these disclosures of my adventures and sometimes hilarious escapades during a life among the sinners and the saints, will also show a more human and endearing side to some of our more unapproachable and earnest public figures.

ONE

WHISKY AND ICE – HOW ANN WIDDECOMBE
'CONVERTED' IN A MEDIA FRENZY AND UPSET
THE BISHOPS – FOX HUNTING AND THE MAU MAU –
'SOMETHING OF THE NIGHT'

It was purely by chance that I met the remarkable woman who I now value as one of my closest friends. It happened, like so many of my chance meetings, in a bar. This one was the Pugin Room in the Palace of Westminster.

She is without doubt the most formidable person I have encountered in the Palace of Westminster. A true phenomenon with a unique personality. You would not, willingly, want to cross Ann and would contradict her only at your peril. In the early days of our friendship, virtually all I did, I admit, was to listen. I didn't dare interrupt her until I came to know her a good deal better. If truth were told I think that to begin with I was more than a little frightened of her. And probably, at times, still am.

Ann could be described as a one-woman task force combining the fire and courage and passion of a crusader and the mental wizardry of an Oxford don, with a captivating and quite unexpected and bubbly sense of fun. She was destined, perhaps surprisingly, to become one of my closest confidantes; I have an endearing love for her.

She is also the most notable of all my 'Seedlings', the term invented by Frank (Lord) Longford, to describe my many 'converts' to the Catholic Church.

Ann is a deeply committed Christian. She comes from an evangelical Anglican background and her brother, Canon Malcolm Widdecombe, was actually vicar of St Philip and St Jacob, Bristol – known as 'Pip 'n Jays'. She was educated at Bath Convent boarding school, run by nuns (La Sainte Union Sisters), a traditional Catholic stronghold of discipline, mystery and doctrine. It was there she learnt how to stand up for herself; it undoubtedly had a lasting effect.

It was in 1987 that my guardian angel led Ann over to the table where I was enjoying an early evening drink with Ken Hargreaves, who was Tory MP for Hyndburn from 1983 to 1992. It was a fine, sunny evening and we had a splendid view of the terrace and the River Thames from the most popular Commons bar. Ann, it turned out, was a close friend of Ken's and having spotted him came straight over to our table. After the introductions she ordered a very large Famous Grouse whisky, in a glass topped up with ice, and took a long swallow when it arrived. Her smile went all the way up to her eyes, and she sighed, 'I think I needed that.'

I soon learned that Ann could consume substantial amounts of Famous Grouse whisky – but loathed other brands – and never diluted her drink with water. Her drinking, like her talking, was ever straight.

In those days Ann's hair was deepest black and cut in a severe, trademark Cromwellian, puritan style. Perhaps difficult to recall now since later on she stunned everyone by suddenly and disconcertingly becoming a blonde, still her colour of choice. But today she has finished with dyes. From now on it's Ann – *au naturel*!

It turned out that Ann liked the clergy and also approved of anything strict, and when I explained my background in the Salvation Army and as a Strict and Particular Baptist she clearly warmed to me. I have always been attracted to nonconformists, for I find, for the most part, that conformists are dull and boring and only ever seem to want to talk about committees, structures, mechanisms or documents. Ann definitely does not conform; she is a one off – absolutely her own person and completely devoid of spin. She is, I have come to believe, like a matrix – a complex place in which ideas are shaped and developed.

After that first meeting I came away thinking, 'This is a very unusual lady. She is either going to kill people verbally, or inspire them to great deeds'. Later, I discovered she would do both with equal dedication and enthusiasm.

As a young woman she had been an administrator at the University of London, which she had seemingly handled with ease. She is an awe-inspiring organizer and I believe could, one day, become a splendid Chancellor of a large university. Indeed, it was widely rumoured that she was shortlisted for the Chancellorship of Oxford university – a post now held by my friend Chris Patten.

Ann and Ken Hargreaves, I learned, were members of a sort of unofficial club affectionately known as the Holy Gaggle. The other members were David Alton – a former Chief Whip for the Liberal Party who, at the time of his elevation in July 1997, was the youngest Life Peer – and David Amess, then Tory MP for Basildon and currently MP for Southend. All four are Catholics and leaders in the pro-life movement, opposing abortion and euthanasia and other related 'life-issues'. I became the fifth musketeer.

In common with most of the events in Ann's somewhat turbulent life, her conversion to Catholicism was characteristically dramatic and a media frenzy. It also earned me a severe ticking off from an irate Cardinal Hume.

Ann's views on women priests matched that of many traditional theologians. The argument is complex, yet simple. For Ann, 'God the Father sent His Son, Jesus, human and divine, to teach his Word and Jesus chose only men to be His Apostles. God's choice is good enough for me and should be good enough for the Church of England.'

But, of course, not everyone agreed and on 11th November 1992 the Church of England General Synod voted – by a majority of only two – to bring in the ordination of women priests the following year. It almost didn't happen this way as two members of the Synod, both staunchly opposed to the ordination of women were delayed on a train from Brighton (a hotbed of High Church Anglican observance) and therefore were unable to vote on the matter. But as Lady Bracknell observed, the line is immaterial.

Elsewhere in this book, I allude to the enormous impact of that decision on the Catholic Church, but its impact on Ann was no less devastating. She believed that a male-only priesthood was something very special and very sacred and she just couldn't stomach the change. She sought Reception into the Catholic Church. Ann set a date of Wednesday, 21 April 1993 for her 'conversion' (as it is commonly called) and she would have liked it to have been in the chapel in Parliament. But because this was in a palace, was the Queen's chapel, that day happened to be the Queen's birthday and as Ann was a Minister of the Queen, the Cardinal ruled it would cause too much furore and controversy and that I should change the date or change the venue – or ideally both. I should have paid heed, but I didn't. As a compromise, it was agreed that Ann would be Received into the Catholic Church in the Crypt of Westminster Cathedral at 7am on the date set. As a kindness, the Cardinal agreed that I could give her a Catholic Mass in the Parliamentary chapel that evening.

The Cardinal had said a Mass in the Common's Chapel fifteen years earlier and had been splattered with red paint by one of the Reverend Ian Paisley's supposed supporters. But the celebration of Mass by the Cardinal had set a precedent and Catholics were given permission to use the Chapel for Mass by the then Black Rod, the late Admiral Sir Richard Thomas (himself a Catholic) and the then chaplain to the Speaker, Canon Dr Donald Gray, a courtesy which continues to this day.

Ann expected that if word got out, her Reception could turn into a 'three-ringed circus', and she wanted the occasion to be a private and modest affair, with only a few people present. Only a handful of people joined us. David Alton and Julian Brazier, the Catholic Tory MP for Canterbury (standing in for John Patten, then Secretary of State for Education), were Ann's sponsors; Ken Hargreaves and David's PA, Christopher Graffius, were also present.

On reflection, my biggest tactical error about that day was in asking my good friend, Father Norman Brown, a blind priest, to guard the door of the Crypt to make sure nobody came in during the service. We had known the media were hovering about the Cathedral as Ann had issued a press statement that she would give interviews on the Piazza in front of Westminster Cathedral at 8am following her Reception.

The previous night's television news and that morning's papers had carried the story of her 'conversion'. Of course, in the event, it didn't take the Fleet Street hacks long to find out that something was going on in the Crypt and when they couldn't get to us through the Cathedral, they quickly discovered a back way in near the Choir School playground on Ambrosden Avenue.

I had barely launched into the service when there came a great hammering on the Crypt door. Father Norman unfortunately made the mistake of opening the door a chink – but of course, being blind couldn't see who was there. Before he could utter a question as to who was there, he was flung aside as over forty reporters and photographers and TV cameramen, French, Dutch and Germans among them, were through, and had us surrounded at the altar. Father Norman, regaining his composure, sought to ask who these intruders were – though sadly in his confusion, addressed his question to a cupboard full of relics rather than the assembled journalists.

Ann, looking quite serene in her little blue hat and blue dress, clearly wanted the liturgy to proceed and told me to continue despite the intrusion. All that was required of her at the service was for her to say 'I believe and profess all that the Holy Catholic Church reveals, teaches and professes as revealed by

God'. But Ann chose to add some words of her own – 'And I accept all the teachings of Pope John Paul the Second and all his Successors and the Magisterium [authority] of the Church'. What could I say? Sadly, these words are not even uttered by candidates for ordination!

I then preached a little sermon and she knelt down and I confirmed her by invoking the Holy Spirit and applying the sacred Oil of Chrism, and she was 'done'. Not only had she been received into Communion with the Catholic Church, but during the whole event, the cameras never stopped clicking or the bulbs flashing and one could say she was also received by the media! Ann carried on giving interviews all day, and I hoped that by the evening the media would have been satisfied. But when we arrived at the Parliamentary chapel they were again there en masse to greet us.

I had billed the occasion as a special Easter celebration and proposed simply to incorporate Ann's first Mass as a Roman Catholic into the service. However, word had got out as to what was to happen and over 200 people were packed into the chapel. Ann's brother Canon Widdecombe had come up from Bristol, and wore his Anglican robes to say prayers and do a reading.

I believe I used the first incense that had ever been burned in the chapel since Tudor times – though in the process managed to set off the fire alarm. This, of course, alerted the Parliamentary police and the already packed Chapel was suddenly inundated with police officers. The other bell, which we were alerted to by one of the Doorkeepers from the House of Lords, was for a vote in the Upper House.

We sang the hymn Faith of our Fathers, Ann's favourite, and

in honour of the Queen's birthday, the National Anthem. Then fifteen of us went for dinner in the Churchill Room, a room in the Houses of Parliament used for celebrations. The then Prime Minister, John Major, had sent a very friendly, handwritten note to Ann (who was his Pensions Minister), which was read out at the table.

I ought to have realized the amount of publicity Ann's Reception would attract and known that it was simply impossible to keep that kind of event secret. In hindsight, I should also have been more sensitive to other issues within the Catholic Church on that date before agreeing it with Ann. Not to have done so turned out to have been a catastrophic mistake. Diplomatically I was hung out to dry. In just twenty-four hours, I had focused the rage of every single Catholic bishop in England and Wales on myself – not to mention the very personal rage of Cardinal Hume. I was so wrapped up in Ann's Reception, I had completely forgotten about the Catholic Bishops of England and Wales annual Low Week meeting, the week after Easter, during which they would be debating several highly significant and controversial events, including their response towards the inauguration of women priests into the Church of England.

On the day of Ann's Reception, the bishops had agreed a number of important and sensitive statements which were due to be issued two days later, on the Friday, and they were confident the statements, because of their content, would receive widespread press and media coverage. Instead, because of my *faux pas*, Ann's Reception overshadowed everything they had hoped to achieve. In the event, the bishops' conclusions received virtually no coverage. I can see how extremely embarrassing this was for the Cardinal, who felt he had to apologize to the bishops. As an Anglican terrorist I could not have done a better job of torpedoing their collective endeavour.

In turn, I felt I should make some explanation and write a letter asking for their forgiveness. The Bishop of Plymouth, Christopher Budd, kindly set it in front of their places at dinner that night. But for the Cardinal forgiveness, I discovered, did not always begin at home.

I was summoned to the Cardinal's study and given a blistering telling off. Words like 'idiot', 'irresponsible', 'reprehensible' and 'downright bloody stupid' were all contained in his tirade and I was convinced I was about to be sacked. Then, when his anger seemed to be at its peak and he was red in the face, he suddenly stopped. 'And tell Miss Widdecombe I am delighted to welcome her into the Church,' he said. 'Now get out and don't let me catch sight of you for at least a week!'

Having very strong opinions, Ann is rarely upset when someone speaks against her. But she was thoroughly alarmed when members of her own constituency condemned her for her views and began moves to deselect her. In 1995, at the height of the anti fox-hunting controversy, only six Tory MPs supported a ban; Ann, who was violently opposed to the sport, was one of them. However her difficulty in this was that the vast majority of her constituency, Maidstone and The Weald, were just as passionately in favour.

A sufficient number summoned her for a face-to-face hearing with her Constituency Association for her deselection as their MP. It was the first time I had ever seen Ann, who was then a

Home Office minister, really rattled. Politics were her life, and for her to have been dumped by her Constituency and thrown out of Parliament would have been her worst nightmare. To me it seemed like an excellent time for her friends to rally round and give her some support. I discussed it with David Alton and suggested to him that we ask Miles, the Duke of Norfolk, to write a letter to the chairman of her Constituency to be read out before the meeting.

The Duke and I were firm friends and I knew that he was a strong supporter and admirer of Ann, and even though I also knew him to be a great champion of fox-hunting, I believed he would help. Miles didn't hesitate. Yes he would do it, and with the greatest pleasure, but added, 'You and Alton must draft the letter.'

The two of us struggled through most of one evening to prepare the letter, repeatedly altering phrases and words until we were both satisfied the tone and content were right. At which point, unbeknownst to us, Miles decided to do a partial rewrite.

Ann confided to me before the meeting that she was extremely tense, and no wonder. She knew that her constituents were mainly committed country folk and that their support for fox-hunting was both traditional and emotional. As their representative in Parliament she was aware that she had chosen to vote, on their behalf, in a direction that would not have had their majority support. But she could not vote against her conscience. That is, in my opinion, one of Ann's strongest points; she is a potent and resilient force for what she sees as the moral right.

But from the mutterings and looks from her constituents in the meeting hall that night, her moral certitude had brought her a good deal of trouble. Like the huntsmen they supported, this mob was clearly out for blood. And it was Ann's they were after.

On the night, she was confined, alone, in a small room to the side of the stage and waited there, nervously, expecting to be called out and put on the spot right from the start – and mauled from all sides. But when the chairman called the meeting to order he surprised her, and the braying mob, by saying he was going to read out a letter from one of fox-hunting's greatest supporters – the Duke of Norfolk. I cannot remember every word of the letter, but it went something like this:

> Now is the time for us to unite against the terrible enemy which is New Labour. Fighting this creature, which we know as New Labour, is akin to fighting the Mau Mau in Kenya. Here is our common enemy and Ann Widdecombe's opposition to the hunt is a minor matter compared with the real fight against this insidious adversary. She is an exceptional weapon in the battle and now is the time to give her your support. You know my own great affection for hunting. I would not lightly speak against it. But we can always return to our country ways and fight in favour of hunting after we are victorious against New Labour – which I firmly believe could annihilate our society.'

End of meeting. Ann was called on stage and the mob cheered and applauded and she didn't even have to speak or answer a single question.

I have always believed that it was the emotive use of the words 'Mau Mau' which did the trick. The Duke had been a Major-General in Kenya during the Mau Mau insurgency in the fifties and it was the worst image he could conjure up for his listeners. Comparing New Labour to those tribal killers was a bit extreme, but Miles's addition to the letter written by David Alton and me had certainly stirred the hearts and feelings of the people of Maidstone and The Weald that night. They were unanimous in wanting to retain their MP, Ann Widdecombe.

It was only later that Miles revealed that not all the amended words were his. He said one evening he had sought the views of his long-time butler, a more than lifelike Jeeves. And so it was the next morning that not only were Miles's shoes polished and newspaper ready, but a tweaked text of the letter awaited the Duke's approval.

I have often wondered since how her constituents might have reacted had they known that in her home Ann's most cherished set of table mats depict Victorian scenes of fox-hunting! Tally ho!

I have noted over the years that only one thing (other than parliamentary deceit, injustice and pro-life opponents) can be guaranteed to stir feelings of anger and disgust in Ann. That is the neglect or ill-treatment of animals – particularly dogs. I am sure it is one such incident, involving Gordon Brown, which originally coloured her judgement on the Prime Minister.

We were sitting in a tiny alcove which connects the Commons' dining room to the outside terrace, a spot much favoured by small groups of MPs who want to chat – or plot – in private. Ann had invited me, two other priests and a bishop to take supper with her in the Churchill Room, and we were enjoying an apéritif, when around the door popped a familiar face. It was Lucy, the friendly black Labrador who was the then Home Secretary David Blunkett's guide dog. The next face to appear was David's. 'Hello Lucy,' said Ann and reached out a hand. Hearing a familiar voice, David let go his grip of the guide handle, which was attached to a harness on Lucy's shoulders and back, but retained a hold on the leash, allowing Lucy to reach Ann and enjoy some ear fondling.

The next face to appear around the door, and above that of David Blunkett, was that of the then Chancellor, Gordon Brown, shortly followed by the head of the then Foreign Secretary, Jack Straw. The three of them had clearly been hoping to find the area vacant to pursue whatever private discussion they were involved in. But when Gordon saw Ann and the rest of us sitting there, he gripped David's shoulder and firmly steered him and Jack Straw away from us. This had the immediate and unintentional effect of tightening the collar around poor Lucy's neck and she was jerked away from Ann's caress with a sudden yelp.

As the trio vanished with Lucy in tow, Ann was outraged and, in her own dry way, told us she was all for calling the RSPCA. 'How dare he be so un-caring?' I have never heard her speak in favour of Gordon Brown since that incident.

Not all the trouble Ann became embroiled in was of her own making, though, it must be said, she was often more than willing to go halfway to meet trouble, head on. With utter certainty I can say that one of her principal problems came in the rather lean frame of former Tory minister and one time party leader Michael

Howard. It was certainly not the third secret of Fatima that Ann and Michael did not exactly see eye-to-eye. In fact, their relationship deteriorated to such a point that Ann's view of the then Home Secretary was, depending on her mood, often akin to that shared by the cartoonists of the day, who portrayed Michael as everything from a vampire bat to the devil incarnate!

One incident latterly in John Major's Government, explains much. Ann had been appointed as the Minister for Prisons working to Michael Howard. In 1996, the practice of the Prison Service to shackle the most serious or violent women offenders to their beds during childbirth or labour emerged in the media. Looking at it from the question of resourcing, the Government's then view was that to guard one, unrestrained woman, in hospital would take three shifts of two guards which would be expensive and a drain on manpower.

However, the media said the practice of shackling was medieval and blamed Ann for introducing it. *The Daily Mirror* dubbed her Doris Karloff (after Boris, the famous English actor who played Frankenstein's monster and other grisly roles in early horror films).

I had not had an opportunity to discuss the matter with Ann until after Sunday Mass one evening on the steps outside Westminster Cathedral. I suggested, in what I hoped would be a helpful and caring way, 'Why not attach them to their beds with thirty-foot chains so they could at least go to the lavatory unsupervised?' To say that she was not amused would be putting it lightly.

'You would like to see me lynched!' she cried.

The reality was that the policy of shackling had been

established long before Ann became the minister responsible, but she took full responsibility for the practice and the vilification that went with it – even managing to poke fun at the media, she told me, by answering her telephone to them: 'Doris Karloff speaking'. Ann's view was that a simple word of explanation from Michael Howard might have stopped her becoming the most unpopular woman in Britain at the time.

It was around then that Ann asked me to go with her to the Home Office and perform a special blessing. It needed something strong she told me, to be done in her favourite language of Latin. What she really wanted, it transpired, was not an ordinary blessing but a form of Exorcism.

Although not fully convinced of her reasoning, I decided the course of least resistance was to assist (although I am not a recognised Exorcist). Clearly Exorcism is not a rite in very regular use within the Church – thank God! – so I asked another of my 'Seedlings' – those I had received into the Church – who was then studying Theology at Heythrop College, to find some suitable prayers.

He rooted around in the basement of the Catholic Central Library, then based in the Friary building where I lived, and emerged triumphant with the relevant liturgical texts which have remained unaltered for centuries. Even the Bishops of the world gathered at the Second Vatican Council in the early 1960s feared to alter the ritual of Exorcism, lest the Devil be insulted. Better to stick with the devil you know and all that. In the end, in this case, I opted for a blessing with holy water.

Ann's dislike of Michael Howard had already become focussed a year earlier, in October 1995, when Michael sacked Derek

Lewis, the former head of the Granada Group, who had been appointed Director General of Prison Services.

Ann was very concerned about how Michael Howard had informed the Commons about the extent of his involvement in the decision to remove John Marriott, the governor of Parkhurst prison following a mass breakout there. Derek Lewis had wanted to move Marriott to another job but Michael, it was reported, had ordered Lewis to dismiss him and threatened to overrule him if he didn't.

Their disagreement over the Home Secretary's role in the affair bubbled on until October that year when, after reading the results of an enquiry, he called in Derek Lewis and fired him on the spot, despite a strong defence of his position by Ann. 'The way he did it was brutal,' she later told me.

Derek Lewis and his wife were both close friends of Ann. They are committed Christians and Ann adored the family and would go up and stay with them at a croft they owned in Scotland. They were favoured guests at her birthday parties and, later, at her book launches. Derek is suave and charming and exceptionally intelligent – the characteristic in a person that is always most appealing to Ann.

Ann was deeply upset by Derek's sacking and she had, for days, seriously considered resigning in protest over his dismissal. She discussed it with me on several occasions.

She had support in her opinions about Michael from her Ministerial predecessor, Sir Peter Lloyd, who claimed Lewis had suffered a gross injustice and had said that Howard should have backed him, not sacked him, for the huge improvements in security he had brought about. In the end, as we know, Ann chose not to resign, but lost her job anyway eighteen months later when Tony Blair swept to power in the General Election of May 1997.

Having lost the election, John Major resigned as leader of the Conservative Party, and a cluster of ambitious MPs proffered themselves for the vacancy. Among these was Michael Howard, who needless to say was not, in Ann's opinion, the most suitable man for the job. At the time she said she would support any one of the other candidates, but would make it her business to make sure that he did not succeed.

A bare-knuckle fighter in the political ring, Ann was ready for a bruising contest. She consulted me on several occasions about what she should do as she felt it was her moral duty to expose him in relation to his sacking of Derek Lewis. But was aware that there would be strong retaliation and she was ready for it.

One of Michael Howard's alleged supporters told the *Daily Mail* that Derek Lewis had wooed Ann with flowers, chocolates over various dinners. 'I think she fell in love with him; he flattered her vanity,' one asserted. 'I don't think she was used to that, poor girl.'
Accusing Ann of having romantic feelings for Derek Lewis caused her a great deal of upset, especially when her one and only love affair – which is more than widely reported – had been with a fellow Oxford undergraduate when she was young and had waist-length, dark, tumbling hair; the romance had fizzled out after three years. Since then, she says she has preferred hot baths, strong whisky and detective novels to romantic encounters. Michael Howard was quick to state that he was appalled by the *Daily Mail* revelations.

17

The attack on her had been a serious misjudgment by someone though, because it made Ann madder than I have ever seen her. Her only lunch dates with Lewis had been after his dismissal, she declared. Flowers had been sent, but from her to Louise Lewis, his wife, on the day of his sacking. For this, Ann says, she was 'severely reprimanded' by Michael Howard.

'As for chocolates,' she said, 'nobody, especially my friends, woos me with chocolate. They have too much respect for the width of my figure.'

A few days before her damning speech to the Commons about the Michael Howard / Derek Lewis incident, Michael was interviewed by Jeremy Paxman on *Newsnight*, where Michael claimed that the verbal attacks on Ann had not come from his team. But when Paxman asked if Michael had put pressure on Derek Lewis to suspend John Marriott and threatened to overrule him if he didn't, Howard prevaricated. In what has now become one of television's most memorable moments, Paxman asked the same question twelve times – not fourteen times as is oft quoted – and each time Howard failed to answer. The day after the *Newsnight* interview, Ann left a message on her answerphone, 'For anybody tempted to vote for Michael Howard, last night's *Newsnight* should be compulsory viewing'.

Then she went in for the kill.

Having been denied the opportunity to make a personal statement to the House by the then Speaker, Betty Boothroyd, about the sacking of Derek Lewis or to speak in an adjournment debate on the same subject, she finally found an opportunity during the debate on aspects of the Queen's Speech (dealing with the Home Office) on 19 May 1997 – the Labour administration had swept to power at the beginning of the month. She opened with a tribute to Jack Straw, who had been appointed Home Secretary, indicating that it would 'probably be the nicest thing that I shall say to [the Labour Party] for the rest of this Parliament' and then, building up a head of steam, methodically laid out her case against Michael Howard over the sacking of Derek Lewis.

Her forty-minute speech was forensic and devastating and subsequently dubbed by the media as 'the most savage attack ever seen in the Commons'.

Howard's biggest problem was, she said, that his first reaction to attack was denial and semantic prestidigitation. She then added her most devastating remark: 'Howard,' she said, 'has something of the night about him.' Ann had played an important role in derailing Michael in the leadership contest. The phrase also earned her a place in the *Oxford Dictionary of Political Quotations*; it was a true showstopper and the media loved it. Particularly the cartoonists. For with his habitual pinstripe suits, five o'clock shadow, toothy grin and Transylvanian ancestry the Dracula connotation fitted the Howard image to perfection, they acclaimed.

But Ann's idea for her 'something of the night' remark was not entirely original. I know she had had these images of a dark side to Howard for months, but they were brought into focus by a most unlikely third party, the late Frank Longford – a man Ann found difficult to like and who she considered to be completely eccentric. And I was present on both occasions when Lord Longford, the seventh Earl, sowed the seeds of that phrase in Ann's mind.

I had known the two of them for almost a decade when I finally engineered their first meeting, at Frank's request, for lunch in the House of Lords' dining room. He was, it's true, a wonderful and holy eccentric, but underneath the persona of a bumbling old fool there was an extremely keen mind. He knew exactly what he was doing and many people discovered too late and to their detriment that they had underestimated him.

Frank Longford, a tireless campaigner who believed nobody was beyond redemption, had written to Ann on numerous occasions urging her to visit his 'little friends' in prison. These 'little friends' included the Moors Murderers, Myra Hindley and Ian Brady, and Dennis Neilson, the serial killer.

Ann repeatedly refused to meet Frank and finally I told her, 'Whatever you think of him, he is the senior Knight of the Garter, a former government minister and a very distinguished person. You may disapprove of him but I do think you ought to meet him.' She capitulated and in March, 1996 – possibly just to shut me up – she had agreed to a lunchtime meeting. It was to be the lunch from hell.

Before lunch, I almost pleaded with Frank: 'Will you please *not* mention any of your "little friends", particularly Myra Hindley! The best thing you can do is to get to know Ann and not be forceful.' I should have known it was like talking to a brick wall.

On that fateful day I waited in the Peers' Lobby with Frank, and Ann came striding from the Central Lobby along the connecting corridor. She had with her the late Baroness (Emily) Blatch, then a Minister of State for Education. Emily, the hard-working Conservative Peer and staunch evangelical Christian, was usually full of charm; I thought this could bode well for the encounter. Emily was a no-nonsense sort of person, once described as a 'formidably effective performer: articulate, fluent and fast on her feet'; on this occasion, she became merely a spectator and said little...

Frank and Ann had never met before and I introduced them; Frank didn't offer his hand and she didn't offer hers. Then we all walked through to the House of Lords' Dining Room in silence. I walked ahead with Emily, as we prepared ourselves to become joint referees in the impending clash of personalities. It raised quite a stir among the other diners as we trooped in. A most unlikely group: Frank Longford, Emily Blatch, Ann Widdecombe and me. Everyone stared and not a word was spoken as we sat down. There was a strong air of expectancy – like before a major event, such as a tennis final. Frank served first.

That morning the newspapers had carried a story quoting Tony Blair as saying it was not possible to be both a Tory and a Christian. 'I agree with Mr Blair that it is impossible to be a Tory and a Christian,' growled Frank, turning to Ann who was sitting next to him. Emily and I sat facing them. Bad start I thought, as Ann exploded with a strong backhand:

'How dare you say that! It's ridiculous. We *are* the party of the Christians. Your lot are the communists.'

Back came the ball.

'Rubbish,' snapped Frank. 'It's quite obvious to me that it's not possible to be a Tory and a Christian. Mr Blair has got it right.'

I could see that Ann was already on the verge of getting up and going, even before we had ordered our lunch. Her tiny hands were clenched into fists and she had a look of thunder on her face. I said, 'Ann, the menus. What shall we all have?' and burbled on about the weather, forthcoming events at the Cathedral, anything to smooth things down and stop the unstoppable.

I could also see that Frank wasn't interested in anything I was saying; he was in to win this particular set and was just waiting for me to stop chattering so he could fire off his next serve. I hoped Emily might help me out, but she had obviously adopted the stance of a linesperson and didn't say a word. Somehow I managed to keep talking while we ordered our food and struggled through our first course. Ann grimaced across the table at me with an 'I told you so' sort of look on her face, rolling her eyes and winking. I finally ran out of small talk just as the main course arrived.

Frank seized his moment and pounded a killer serve across the table. 'I wish you would visit my prisoners. You never visit them when they write to you.'

Ann responded, 'What prisoners?'

'Myra Hindley,' he bellowed.

Silence in the Peers' Dining Room.

'I will never visit that evil woman. How dare you ask me to do such a diabolic thing,' she hissed.

'But she's requested visits from you.'

Ann's voice started to rise. 'I don't care if she's requested visits. I will never visit her! Don't even think of asking me again.'

Frank, not wishing to miss an opportunity, hit a skilful drop shot. 'What about Fred West?'

This was, on reflection, not perhaps the smartest or most graceful shot of Frank's.

'Don't dare continue on this line another moment. I am not interested in any of your evil monsters; they should all have been hanged!' Ann's views on capital punishment are well known and she has never been exactly delicate in discussing it.

Everyone in the room seemed to be waiting for the next volley. But Frank suddenly decided to switch subjects with a gentle backhand: 'How on earth can you work with that man Michael Howard?' he asked, making the sign of the cross over himself as he did so. 'You must know he is the Prince of Darkness,' and he blessed himself again. This was safer ground.

Ann certainly wasn't going to disagree with him about this. She disliked the Home Secretary almost as much as our host appeared to, though without the full satanic trappings. And as Longford continued his diatribe against her boss I actually began to believe that Ann was warming to him, and that we might make it to the end of lunch.

In the end, her bleeper went off and further volleys were avoided. I remain convinced she had a trick of sending a signal when she wanted to receive a bleep and escape a situation; she probably thought it didn't look right for her to sit there listening to Longford loudly running down her immediate boss without defending him. She looked up from her bleeper and said curtly, 'I've got to go,' and she rose to her feet and walked away, without bothering to say goodbye to Frank, simply nodding in his direction.

I breathed a sigh of relief. At least it hadn't all ended in *total* disaster. Then Frank himself wandered off, also without saying goodbye, and I had to dash after him, because he was our host and as usual he hadn't paid for lunch. He settled the bill at the bar and that was it. He had had his say about his little friends to Ann and wasn't interested in finishing his lunch. Emily and I remained. The tennis between Frank and Ann had rendered her utterly speechless and only with the departure of our more volatile companions did she mumble her first words. So ended the lunch from hell; but it was not the end of the Longford / Widdecombe saga.

A few weeks after that initial meeting, Longford asked if he could meet Ann again. I almost laughed out loud. But he was serious. He realized, he told me, he had overstepped the mark on the first occasion and he promised that if she would agree to another lunch, he would not mention his 'little friends' again. He was genuinely one of her great admirers, he said. I didn't hold out much hope but Ann surprised me by saying, 'I don't like the man at all, but I do admire his daughter and I like her work.'

Lady Antonia Fraser had just written a book, *The Gunpowder Plot – Terror and Faith in 1605*, which Ann had read and thoroughly enjoyed. I told Frank that if he could arrange for his daughter to be there, then Ann would agree to another lunch. Ann and Antonia hit it off tremendously well almost immediately and most of our time together was spent talking about Antonia's books.

But the most fascinating, and amusing, anecdote during lunch came from Frank himself. He revealed that he had never actually met Michael Howard, 'Having had no wish to confront such evil face to face,' he said. Frank had been invited to a function at 10 Downing Street and by accident had bumped into the then Home Secretary. 'Imagine it. I didn't even recognize him close up,' he said. 'But suddenly I was confronted by this man and I said "Who are you?" to which he of course replied, "I'm Michael Howard".'

'It was an awful shock,' said Lord Longford. He said that he had exclaimed 'The Prince of Darkness!' and crossed himself over and over again. Howard, it transpired, had stared at Longford as the peer rushed out of the room.

The day following Howard's demise Frank insisted on a meeting with Ann.

'So she finally realized he was the Prince of Darkness,' he chortled. 'Widdecombe is a very special woman.'

We secretly found the story very amusing, picturing Frank meeting a bemused Michael Howard. I am quite certain that it was because of his remarks about Howard being 'the Prince of Darkness' that her 'something of the night' phrase began to take shape in her mind. I didn't share Frank's conviction that Michael Howard was in cahoots with the devil, and nor do I – thank goodness! – have Frank's ability of being so relentlessly blunt.

I had previously dined with Michael Howard and his beautiful wife Sandra at a dinner party hosted by Alan Clark, and genuinely enjoyed the company of this highly distinguished politician, regardless of others' opinions. But with all that had passed, our next encounter was so much harder to cope with.

It was just a few days after Ann's famous speech about Michael in the Commons, that circumstances brought us together again following the annual parliamentary tug-of-war. By then the press had probed Ann's motives for her attack and sensationally 'revealed' that her priest, Father Michael Seed, had 'told her to do it'. Michael Howard could not have escaped seeing the headlines nor reading the press version of my supposed role in his downfall – something which is not true.

However, on the walk from Abingdon Green, where the tug-of-war had taken place, to the grounds of Westminster Abbey, where there was to be a reception and dinner, I became separated from my hostess and suddenly found myself walking next to Michael and Sandra Howard. Thinking of their sensitivities, I wished with all my heart that this encounter was not happening at that time and was cross with myself for not having spotted them earlier and taken evasive action. But in that enormous crowd I didn't dream that we might end up together. He was, of course, very polite and civil and seemed quite calm even though the events of the last days were uppermost in both our minds they were never mentioned. I can't for the life of me remember a single thing we talked about and I know there were some long silences. On reflection, perhaps our meeting was providential but I was exceptionally thankful when we reached the marquee.

It was always Ann's intention to resign from Parliament after the next general election, but as we go to print there seems to be a chink in her armour. The issue of a vacant, very large chair in the chamber of the Commons – seeking a new Speaker.

In light of this, dear Ann, I am informed, is wobbly on the issue of staying or going.

A goodly number of people are forming unholy alliances to try and make sure than Ann is comfortably seated on the green leather of the Speaker's chair. The day they have chosen for the election could not be more appropriate for Ann as Monday 22nd June is the feast day of a former Speaker, Sir Thomas More – who preferred to serve God more than King Henry VIII.

Saint Thomas, as he became, is one of Ann's heroes, as, like her, he stood entirely for truth and integrity – even giving his life for his beliefs.

TWO

TUG-OF-WAR BY THE RIVER – DIRTY TRICKS AT
ST PAUL'S – GERMAN BUILDERS VERSUS THE
HOUSEHOLD CAVALRY – BANNED FOR CHEATING –
PALACE OF VARIETIES

Since 1988, a charity tug-of-war competition has been held
every year in June, on Abingdon Green, Westminster, next to
the Jewell House and opposite the Victoria Tower of the Houses
of Parliament, the highlight of which is the fiercely contested
battle between members of the Commons and members of the
Lords. The ribald cries from some of our most famous politicians,
urging on their participant colleagues in their whites and trainers
– usually far wittier than their comments in the two Houses –
with all participants going red in the face trying to out-tug or out-
goad their opponents, provides some rare entertainment.

It is a huge social event attracting hundreds of MPs and Lords
and others, and raises funds for the Macmillan Cancer Support. In
the nineties, the event was organized by Eira Jessel, wife of the then
Conservative MP for Twickenham, Toby Jessel, who lost his seat to
a Liberal Democrat in 1997, after twenty-five years. There is always

a lively drinks party beforehand in the grounds of Westminster Abbey and a more formal dinner there afterwards. I had often attended as a guest and always found it to be enormous fun.

Several other bouts are also pulled at each event, and on the particular year I recall, involved a cut-throat contest between clerics of the Abbey and St Paul's Cathedral. When Eira Jessel, herself a Catholic, suggested that Westminster Cathedral might challenge a team from St Paul's, I didn't hesitate to accept the contest on the spot. I reasoned that we had plenty of stalwart priests with bell-pulling experience and extremely generous girths to provide sufficient dead weight to prevent St Paul's pulling us off our base. But that's before I heard about our opponents' 'dirty tricks' department. It appeared St Paul's was undergoing a massive conservation programme and they had a goodly supply of huge and muscular German builders working on the site. Word was that these Germanic strongmen were to form the backbone of the Anglican Cathedral's team.

In the mid-nineties, I was still the official Catholic Chaplain at London's Wellington Barracks and lost no time in contacting the regimental sports instructor – a sergeant major, no less! We needed both their training tips and a supply of British beefcake to cope with the dastardly Deutschen, I told him. That weekend four large Grenadier Guardsmen and their fierce-looking drill instructor arrived at the Cathedral with about fifty metres of very thick rope. I had already assembled a group of the biggest, strongest and fittest priests (and a few laymen and women), I could find in the Cathedral and Archbishop's House, and found that eight of these could just about hold their own against the four Guardsmen.

At the end of that first session the priests were exhausted. It was clear that, for many of them, when just the thought of exercise popped into their heads, they would sit down until it passed. Still, I noticed we had attracted a sizeable crowd of the Cathedral's female secretarial staff and nuns who enthusiastically applauded the exertions of the young soldiers in their brief shorts and singlets. They came three times in all and after each training session we all gathered for drinks in the Cathedral Clergy House or the local pub, appropriately called The Cardinal.

Just one week before the actual contest I heard from my spy in St Paul's Cathedral that they intended fielding an incredible eight German workers in their team. The answer seemed obvious. The Grenadiers' instructor concurred that he and the four Guardsmen should become honorary priests for the day. I prayed for God's forgiveness, but figured He must have known about the St Paul's deceit as well. It was still a disaster. With little more than one mighty pull the St Paul's German builders dragged our struggling priests and Guardsmen over the marker – where they all fell in a tangled heap.

I was determined that the same thing shouldn't happen twice and the following year I switched from the Grenadiers to the Houschold Cavalry, five very tough-looking young men from the Knightsbridge barracks. I thought with them and with a little help from my priests, we would see off the Germans.

I should have learned my lesson the first time. The Cavalry were worse than the Guards. They weren't at all happy losing – especially to the Germans – but after their assurances beforehand, they really had no-one to blame but themselves. I should have copied the St Paul's team and put eight ringers into my side. Sadly, I wasn't to be given a third opportunity to test my theory. Word about our cheating had somehow emerged and both St Paul's and Westminster Cathedral were banned from fielding a team at future events.

Another regular fund-raising event for Macmillan, the *Parliamentary Palace of Varieties* show, initially held at the splendid St John's, Smith Square never lacks for volunteers. Show them any stage or platform on which to perform and it is likely that most MPs and Lords will rush forward, *en masse*. As Michael Billington, the Arts Critic for *The Guardian* once observed, 'While it occasionally has the air of a staff concert in which the geography teacher lets his hair down, it reminds us that politicians are, by definition, born performers.'

Sometimes though there are some real stars amongst them, the big hit in 2008 being maverick Labour MP Bob Marshall-Andrews, performing a wickedly funny monologue as a heavily Irish-accented priest from Westminster Cathedral, recounting the first confession he had taken from a well-known recent convert to Catholicism.

But the biggest show stopper came from the Whips and their staffs – the highlight being a rendition of Tom Lehrer's *Masochism Tango* when they dropped their robes to reveal an array of leather, chains and other accoutrement usually associated with Soho, loaned I was told, by Baroness [Genista] McIntosh of Hudnall.

With the lights dimmed, the robes discarded, and the opening lines of the *Tango* sung by the assembled company – *I ache for the touch of your lips, dear / but much more for the touch of your whips, dear...* – the dancing Whips brought the house down.

Such a polished performance that some members of the audience were moved to suggest that it might well be the result of countless hours of dedicated private rehearsal!

$\mathcal{T}$HREE

MEETING TONY BLAIR – JAMES BOND ANTICS –
CHERIE AND COMMUNION – GORDIE BROWN AT
WORK IN LAS VEGAS – GOING TO WAR IN IRAQ –
DOWNING STREET PLAYPEN

My visits to Downing Street to hold Masses for Tony Blair and his family were never meant to be a secret, nor a way of sneaking the Prime Minister into the Catholic Church via 'the back door' – even if my first visit there was like something out of a James Bond film.

At my request I found myself tiptoeing round to the back of Number 10, clutching a small bag of things I needed for Holy Communion, and climbing clandestinely in through a ground-floor window. For years my visits were as closely guarded as the Cabinet Minutes.

The first time I met Tony, he was sitting between a young prostitute and a homeless addict. I was on the opposite side of the table with his wife, Cherie, at an event I had helped organize to bring together the 'haves and the have-nots'. Tony's table neighbours had no idea who he was, and he had to explain to them just what it is that Her Majesty's Leader of the Opposition does. A long and lively conversation ensued as he turned on the full power of his charm and evoked much laughter from the two young guests.

The event, The Big Banquet, as it was billed, took place on the eve of Pentecost in 1995, the year after Tony Blair took over the leadership of the Labour Party, following the untimely death of John Smith. 1995 was the midway point in the Decade of Evangelization, a joint initiative of the late Pope and the then Archbishop of Canterbury, which would conclude with the celebration of the third millennium of the birth of Christ in 2000. To mark this staging post, a series of events to raise awareness of the importance of Christ in the second millennium were proposed which sought to encourage people around the country to have a meal with neighbours, or strangers – even to knock on someone's door and extend the hand of friendship.

The Banquet was the main event in Greater London and four of us had arranged events across the capital including a dinner at the Whitehall Banqueting House: the Reverend Adele Blakeborough; the Reverend Andrew Mawson (now Lord Mawson); Helen Taylor Thompson, an Anglican; and me, from the Catholic Church (who had the honour of obtaining a licence for the consumption of alcohol for the occasion). As a former Salvation Army adherent, I had never previously run a bar, but it is widely thought I have made up for lost time subsequently!

There were many VIPs present, including a representative of the John Major Government, and the then Commissioner of the Metropolitan Police. The country's senior religious leaders were to act as waiters and serve the drinks and hors d'oeuvres – not that it was easy getting the Church leaders into action as most of them were most reluctant to do their assigned tasks; I had to bully them slightly. Archbishop Michael Bowen of Southwark, a saintly man, was not at all comfortable or confident as a waiter, and had retreated into a corner. 'Your Grace, it's time to start serving,' I told him and steered him towards the laden trays of wine and soft drinks.

Soon the Bishop of London, the Salvation Army General, the Moderators of the Methodist, Baptist, United Reformed Church and Cardinal Hume, all in their robes, were circling the reception area with drinks, serving the homeless, the recovering drunks, addicts and prostitutes as well as our better-known guests (with no guarantee, of course, that the latter did not contain various elements of the former among them). The Catholics there, I must admit, made dreadful waiters.

Hume frowned upon the event as he saw it as a gimmick, and he did not like gimmicks; he also disapproved of the cost. Hume was not one to spend money on anything but worthy causes; in the event, the Catholic Church paid £5,000 towards the cost of the events in London, but only after much persuasion.

Several people made speeches including Andrew Mawson and Trevor Phillips, then Head of Current Affairs at London Weekend Television, now Chairman of the Equality and Human Rights Commission. After Phillips claimed in 1996 that the Notting Hill Carnival was not a celebration of multiculturalism but rather of one community's culture, Ken Livingstone made the famous, absurd remark in a live radio interview: 'He's so right wing he'll soon be joining the BNP'.

The Reverend Jesse Jackson, the American human rights and racial equality campaigner, turned up unexpectedly and in the company of an extensive cohort of media people, and made a rather long, seemingly impromptu speech. I felt rather sorry for Trevor since it rather trumped anything which had been said before.

Trevor is a close friend of Peter Mandelson (who was best man at his wedding) and who was also on the next table to ours – though Peter spent most of the meal hovering around Tony Blair, obviously concerned that Tony might be seen in the company of 'sinners'. It was the first time I had actually seen Peter and I distinctly remember wondering at the time whether he actually managed to eat anything...

Ian Hargreaves, then editor of *The Independent*, was on our table and brought up the question of whether a Catholic could become Prime Minister. Interestingly no-one tried to argue that it would not be possible, nor did anyone ask the question of whether a Prime Minister could become a Catholic! I was then unaware of Tony's resolve to one day join the Catholic Church, though naturally knew of his resolve to be our next PM. I didn't realize the significance of Ian's question until years later.

I was surprised to be on the Blairs' table at all, but I thoroughly enjoyed sitting next to Cherie and Trevor. She told me she came from Bury, close to where I went to school in Rochdale; the areas around Manchester and Liverpool where I had been raised were familiar to her.

Then she mentioned the gritty, contemporary film *Priest* that was nominated for a BAFTA, which was highly controversial at the time of its release and which I had reviewed for the oldest

Catholic weekly journal, *The Tablet*. It was about a young priest who struggles with issues around sexuality which contribute to his real struggle of faith. I told her that the bishop in the film had not reacted like any bishop I had ever known.

Cherie told me that her actor father, Tony Booth, and her eldest son, Euan, were in the film. I hadn't known this when I had attended a private showing of *Priest*, as there had been no publicity linking it to the Blairs. It was a very tense, controversial and mature piece of cinema and I was surprised and impressed that she had allowed Euan, who was only ten when it was made, to be in it.

I saw little of them for the next two or three years. Occasionally I would see Tony in Parliament and we would greet one another, but that was all. The family, when in London, went to Mass in St Joan of Arc, in Islington near to where they were living. The whole family played an active part within the parish, such as reading, praying the intercessions and the children serving at the altar. But after Tony became Prime Minister in May 1997, they began attending Mass at Westminster Cathedral each week and we would often stand in the Piazza outside and chat after Mass. There weren't the ultra strict security issues then that developed later and they were still able to interact with others like a normal family. Even so, we never knew in advance when they were coming. It could be on a Saturday evening or to any of the seven Masses that were said on Sundays.

As the priest responsible for confirmation preparation at the Cathedral, I was aware that children were not always there willingly, and sometimes were forced to be confirmed by their parents, or indeed grandparents. So as not to bore the young people, I liked to walk my class of about forty students around the Cathedral while I was teaching, as my perambulating hero, Aristotle, did; they were a pretty unruly bunch and to combat any misbehaviour I avoided sitting them down anywhere! It was a great joy to welcome Euan and later his younger brother, Nicky, to these classes. Some of the other pupils from the distinguished London Oratory School also attended my classes. I suspected that, at times, they could be quite unpleasant to Euan. I'm sure that it was just verbal and nothing physical – boys will be boys – but it made me aware of how difficult it must have been for these two brothers to have the Prime Minister of the day as their father.

The first time I was invited to Downing Street with the Blairs in residence, was on Sunday, May 21st 2000, the day after Leo was born. Cherie had contacted me at the friary when she returned home from hospital and asked if I could go to their flat and administer her Holy Communion. I suggested because of my record in 'converting' people to Catholicism, it might spark gossip that Tony was planning to become a Roman Catholic if I was seen going through the front door in Downing Street. She hadn't considered that aspect at all, and did not seem particularly bothered by it – but said perhaps it would be better if I went in around the back. She instructed me how to get in through a gate off Horse Guards Parade in the side wall of Downing Street, and take a small alley which led to the Prime Minister's garden.

I followed my instructions and came to a half-raised, large sash window, where a security officer in white shirt and black trousers waited to help me climb inside. As I stepped in, clutching my little bag of accessories, I felt as though I belonged in one of those exotic spy movies.

It was the first time I had been inside Downing Street since John Major's departure. Quite a bit had changed, especially with the arrival of tiny feet! Because the Blairs were a large family, and the apartment at Number 11 was much bigger, Tony had put Gordon Brown in the smaller apartment above Number 10 and taken the Chancellor's traditional home for himself – though each man kept his executive offices in the usual building. A large arch had been knocked through the ground-floor wall separating the two residences to make the switch of living accommodation easier.

I was met and guided upstairs by Mrs Blair's mother, Gale, until we came to a closed door on a landing. When we knocked, Cherie called out to enter. I went in alone and found her in bed. She greeted me with a smile, offered me a seat and I was about to give her Holy Communion when Tony bounded in through a second door, wearing his gym kit. He had clearly been exercising and I don't know who was more surprised – him unexpectedly to find a man sitting on his wife's bed, or me to see the Prime Minister of the United Kingdom in such a state!

Confusion over, Cherie ordered Tony off to have a quick shower while I continued Communion with her. When he came back, looking slightly more presentable, I blessed Tony and baby Leo. They had people downstairs still celebrating Leo's birth and he invited me to join them for a glass of champagne. The drawing room was quite crowded. Lord Falconer was there with his wife Marianna, along with Tony's sister, Sarah, plus, of course, Euan, Nicky and Kathryn. Cherie came down to join us and I stayed about an hour. It was a lovely get-together to celebrate a new addition to the family and could have been taking place in almost any home in the country. It was a very cosy, heart-warming scene of real domestic bliss, with much love around.

When the time came to leave it was Tony who showed me downstairs to the front door. I asked him, 'Don't you think I should go out through the back window where I came in? If I'm seen leaving, everyone will think you're my next convert to the wicked Papists.' He laughed nervously, unaware of my clandestine entry. 'Don't worry about that. Let them all think what they like! You're going out through the front door and must come in that way in future.' As it happened, when the policeman let me out through the door of Number 10 with my little bag, the media had all gone home – and it would be six years before anyone would recognize me and break the story of my 'Meals on Wheels' service, which was my code name for the Downing Street Masses.

After the birth of Leo, the Blairs continued to attend Mass at the Cathedral, sometimes Tony or Cherie alone, sometimes together, or sometimes with the children. They acted like any other family of parishioners, sending gifts for the Christmas and summer parish fetes – usually signed bottles of whisky. Every Christmas Tony would place a large collection box for The Passage, a shelter for the homeless (operated within the Westminster Cathedral parish), inside the front door of Number 10, and Sister Ellen, or her predecessor, Sister Bridie, directors of The Passage, would pop in and say Merry Christmas to everyone and collect the donations. There were many, and they were generous.

Then came 9/11 and, sadly, everything changed. For a while

after the terrorist attacks on America the Blairs showed up randomly at different churches all over London. No-one knew where they might pop up. But even that became quite silly and difficult because of the ever increasing security requirements, and eventually it was decided it would be easier and safer for everyone if Mass was celebrated in their own home.

To some people it may have seemed as though they were taking advantage of Tony's privileged position to have the priest go to them, but that was the necessity even if the Blairs, especially Cherie, simply hated not being members of a living Church community. It was the same at Chequers (the country home of the Prime Minister) where Mass was often said by either the local priest, endearing Canon Timothy Russ, or their good friend, Principal RAF chaplain, Monsignor John Walsh.

To begin with, it was usually Mrs Blair who called to arrange these services or sometimes it would be a secretary, or duty clerk, who would leave a message for me to call Number 10. At the start they were very discreet but in time they became much less formal. When I called 'the switch' – the affectionate name for those operating the Number 10 switchboard – they would put me straight through to Cherie or, on rare occasions, connect me directly to the Prime Minister's office. I would always try to deal with Cherie (if I could) or with their special secretary, the delightful Sue Geddes. I would be asked if I could come that day or the following day. It was mostly very last-minute and difficult to plan in advance. They always tried to fit in with what I could do and were never demanding.

Even with the Mass, it was only an hour of my time since I walk so fast that I am quicker than the number 11 or 24 bus going along Victoria Street and round Parliament Square, where the traffic is nearly always atrocious, and I could reach Downing Street in just over ten minutes. We held our little services in the parlour, either on Saturday night or Sunday. The family would sit on a long couch on one side of a coffee table and I would sit on a second, identical, couch facing them. It was very rare for them all to be there as the children often stayed with close friends at weekends.

Often after I had said Mass we would sit and chat. It really depended on how busy they were. On quite a number of occasions, when I arrived early, I found Tony down on his hands and knees playing with Leo. The whole of their apartment was one large playpen for Leo. They didn't seem to restrict him to any one place and his toys – trucks, Lego, blocks, books and miniature figures – were scattered everywhere. I enjoyed watching them play together – the Prime Minister and the toddler. A huge model train layout seemed to be a permanent fixture of the entrance hall and a large play tent was erected in the reception lobby. Postman Pat and Bob the Builder were always around.

In his role as Postman Pat, an office he took very seriously, the toddler would make his way downstairs to where the incoming post was gathered and either ask for or take letters for his family back to the flat. On one occasion I was waiting in a parlour on the ground floor for Mrs Blair, when I saw what looked like an extremely vertically-challenged postman making his way towards the stairs to the flat. It was Leo in his Postman Pat outfit doing what appeared to be his favourite daily family chore – and obviously loving it. Goodness knows what international political hot potatoes were delivered by those tiny, chubby fingers.

Tony and Cherie were determined that, despite the huge pressures on their time, they would always find moments for bonding with their children, and to the best of my knowledge they always did.

After a number of months, I no longer needed to bring Communion wine or my missal with me as I kept a bottle in their drinks cupboard in the corner, along with my holy books. Sadly it wasn't (from my point of view) a heavily stocked cupboard although in the latter days before the 'Scottish Presbyterian invasion' of Number 10 and Number 11, I rescued three bottles, one an extremely fine brandy which I still have for special occasions. Communion wine, often known to us priests as 'gut-rot' is fortified and doesn't usually become sour or go off.

My celebration of Mass at Downing Street was not deliberately concealed, though from the outset I had remained silent about it, except with the Cardinal and other trusted colleagues at the Cathedral. It didn't hit the media until a year before Tony Blair left office, not that it was really the business of any but the family and the Church.

The story broke because Mrs Blair and the children had gone off on a summer holiday, leaving Tony in London to sort out various emergencies, and a parishioner of mine, who could not stand Labour and knew that Tony was there alone, saw me emerging from Number 10 and tipped off the press.

I was upset that the Masses at Number 10 had become public knowledge because of me, but Tony showed no reaction and Cherie, when she learned, was not at all concerned.

On a lighter note, one Sunday in 2004, after I had finished Mass, he inquired of my recent visit to the United States. I told

Tony in a conspiratorial voice, 'I have something very important to tell you.'

He looked slightly apprehensive. 'What is it?'

In a serious voice I replied, 'It involves your Chancellor, Gordon Brown.'

'Oh. Really?' he said, and I could tell I had his full attention.

'Yes, I think he's been earning money in Las Vegas.'

'What!' The Prime Minister was agog to know more.

What I had yet to reveal was my 'discovery' of one 'Gordie Brown', a musician, comedian and entertainer who was appearing at the Golden Nugget, one of the glitzy casinos on the Strip. Being amused by this, I had managed to acquire one of the A4-sized advertising posters from the casino front desk, which I had brought with me in my bag, with the intention of teasing Tony.

I said, 'I thought it only right that you should know. Gordon has been appearing at the Golden Nugget and has made himself up to disguise his true identity.' At this point Tony was staring at me in open-mouthed disbelief and his habitual smile had vanished. 'I'll have to show you,' I said, and produced the poster with a flourish. 'See?!'

He took it in both hands, looked at it very hard for a whole minute, then rolled it up and put it in a drawer and walked out of the room, without speaking. I really thought that the joke had badly misfired and he was probably at that moment calling one of his close friends Alastair Campbell or Peter Mandelson, for advice (or, on the other hand, contacting the police simply to eject me). When Cherie came into the parlour I told her what had happened and that I feared I had genuinely annoyed him. When she took the poster from the drawer she began laughing so much she collapsed on the couch. 'That's priceless,' she giggled, dabbing at her eyes.

Her reaction was very much the same as mine had been, but I was still worrying about Tony's strange response and whether I had hurt his feelings. Suddenly the door swung back and in jumped the Prime Minister, grinning from ear to ear. 'Got you at your own game there, Michael,' he said, and began to shake with laughter. I still can't see Gordon Brown without thinking of his namesake – Gordie, in Las Vegas – and smiling.

One day I was letting myself out of the Blairs' apartment, carrying my small bag, when I encountered Alastair Campbell on his way up to see the Prime Minister. I believe he had been jogging in some marathon or other and was clad only in shorts and a skimpy vest and carrying a little bag of his own. He looked extremely healthy and fit and had lost a lot of weight. It was odd being face-to-face with the very man, the Adonis of New Labour (a role I can imagine was fought over by others) who had very famously quoted to the press, 'We don't do God.'

I had never met him properly but each of us was aware of who the other was. He probably knew everything about me, down to the number on my passport; I knew just a little about him from some of his neighbours in Gospel Oak – in the circumstance, perhaps an ironic place for Alastair to live!

'Father Seed,' he said.

'Alastair,' I replied. 'I've never had the pleasure of meeting you in the flesh before – and what a lot of it you're showing.' That flustered him, so I added, 'I've just been doing God with my little bag of tricks,' and I shook it under his nose. I had always wanted to say that, though I don't think Mr Campbell found it anywhere near as amusing as I did...

Much of the public remain deeply unhappy about the Iraq War and the way the then Prime Minister appeared to lead Britain in support of George W Bush. While this is not the place to debate the rights and wrongs of any war, I think it is apparent that Tony thought and prayed long and hard about how to respond to the atrocities in America on 11 September 2001 and the subsequent developments. In this context, I have seen Tony almost tearful in sadness – most especially at the tragic deaths of our brave service personnel – and full of anger at injustice and, despite enduring constant and unremitting pressure from several forces, did what he truly believed was right, the concern of the Just War Tradition.

I believe there was no element of opportunism in his decision to invade Iraq. There was a serious conviction that it had to be done. Of course he fully understood the consequences of his actions. He knew what would happen – the same as I am convinced he knew that eventually he would be blamed.

I am also absolutely certain that he was not toadying to Bush in any sense. In fact I believe what he was attempting to do was to be a balance for Bush by being involved. He provided a greater objectivity to the war, instead of a prevailing subjectivity of sending more and more troops.

I know that he did not take the decision to go to war lightly. There was no question of it being 'America is our ally so we have to join them'. There was none of the John Wayne, gung-ho element involved. I still believe that if there were lies or evasions then I am certain they did not come from Tony Blair.

In truth, there are a lot of people still in Parliament who regret that he did not stay on. Many were saddened when he left and only a few were truly delighted. They are even fewer now.

One of the few times I saw him particularly low, was after his decision to step aside in favour of Gordon Brown. While there was a certain relief when he finally decided to go, I am convinced he would rather have departed in losing a general election. I was in America when he actually left Downing Street, celebrating my Silver Jubilee of my Life Vows as a Franciscan.

My last Mass with the Blairs in their parlour was on Sunday, 13th of May. On the 17th of May I was appalled to read a front-page story in *The Times* which claimed 'Father Seed confirms that Blair is to become a Catholic'. It covered the whole front page and two pages inside and the story caused a great deal of consternation.

The background to the 'scoop' was very simple: during a reception in the House of Lords following a memorial service for the late Lord Carter, a rather pompous guest had come up to me and asked me if there was anything in the rumour that Tony Blair was to become a Catholic. I gave my standard answer to this question: 'Why don't you telephone Mr Blair and ask him yourself? I have nothing say about the matter.'

However, it transpired the guest had apparently spoken to a third party, who had in turn spoken to Ruth Gledhill, the religious correspondent of *The Times*. A week before the reception, Ruth had telephoned me and said, 'Michael, I have just been told that you have confirmed that Tony Blair is to become a Catholic.'

I said, 'That's absolute nonsense because, as you know, I never discuss it. You cannot quote me at all on this subject because I have nothing to say.'

I thought that was the end of the matter. However, eight days later, the article appeared in *The Times* under her by-line stating that: 'In an interview last night, Father Seed said...'

I only read the article late in the day of its publication after receiving a not very complimentary note in my box – each chaplain at the Cathedral had a box outside the Clergy Common Room to receive external and internal post / messages – from Cardinal Cormac, mentioning my involvement. It was the most upsetting note I ever received from him for he, and others, had immediately assumed that the article in *The Times*, was entirely accurate. This certainly gives weight to the adage never to believe everything you read in a newspaper.

I immediately telephoned Downing Street to discuss the matter with their Press Office, who were most understanding. I then spoke to Ruth. There is little one can really say about that, but no-one needed such speculation circulating in the press, particularly on such an emotive subject. It was not at all helpful for anyone, most especially so for the Cardinal. Subsequently, I received a letter from Cherie Blair which went a long way to help calm down the Cardinal and later that year in July, I bumped into Tony at Wembley Stadium at an event celebrating sport – at which Sir Alex Ferguson made a deeply moving speech about his family's dire poverty when he was growing up, and the value of sport in transforming the lives of 'ghetto kids' from penniless backgrounds.

I was able then to assure Tony that I had spoken to no-one about his faith or possible Reception into the Church. He patted my shoulder and said, 'Michael, don't worry about it. You worry too much. I'm just very grateful for all you have done for me and for my family. These bits and pieces about Masses and so on I don't mind at all, and neither should you.'

I wonder if Mr Blair had wanted to become a Methodist or a Baptist, whether the media would have shown the slightest interest. It's just that Catholics have such a seriously naughty image that people get excited – maybe it is to do with the Catholics' plot to blow up Parliament or the head-lopping excesses of Mary Tudor.

By the time we met at Wembley, Tony's decision to become a Roman Catholic was already an accepted fact in the media, and he was finally received into the Church by Cardinal Cormac in his private chapel in Archbishop's House, on Friday, December 21st the same year.

FOUR

HOW THE DUKE TOLD THE POPE TO CHOOSE BASIL
– MISS PIGGY LENDS A HAND – ARGUMENT IN A
CUPBOARD – TALKING IN TONGUES – A FAMOUS FAT
LADY HITS THE BOTTLE – WOMEN PRIESTS –
THE POPE AND SPITFIRE ALE

Without the powerful intervention of Miles, the late Duke of Norfolk, Basil Hume would probably have remained at Ampleforth Abbey until his death. In November 1975, it appeared to have been decided that the then Bishop of Portsmouth, Derek Worlock, would succeed as the ninth Archbishop of Westminster following the death of the much loved Cardinal Heenan. When Miles, the Earl Marshall of England and the country's premier Catholic peer, chose to intervene, Worlock, he told me, had been approached and had already agreed to take the job.

Derek Worlock had been private secretary to several Cardinal Archbishops at Westminster and although a good, prayerful and intelligent man, was considered by Miles to be grimly serious and rather dull. Miles (whom I knew well until his death in 2002) told me subsequently that in 1975 the

Church desperately needed an inspirational and dynamic personality at the helm.

'I decided that Basil Hume was the right man for the job,' he said. Basil was eight years Miles's junior and had studied at Ampleforth after the Duke. They had become friends long before Hume became Abbot there.

'Basil was head of sports and captain of nearly everything,' said Miles. 'Just the type we needed to shake the doldrums out of the Church and provide some real leadership.'

When he was told that Bishop Worlock had almost certainly been selected, Miles, a powerful man, but utterly devoid of pomposity, refused to accept it.

'It was time to go and talk to the top man,' he told me.

So he went directly to Pope Paul VI in Rome and told him the story of Basil Hume.

'He is the right man for the Church and for the people,' Miles told the Pope. 'On that I will stake my life. We need new blood.'

Miles's prescience was to prove a true blessing for the Catholic Church in England and it was fortunate that the then Holy Father, Pope Paul VI, saw the much larger picture. The Church was already forward-planning a celebration in 1980 to mark the 1,500 years since the birth of St Benedict and he had been advised at the time there were currently no Benedictine cardinals and that Basil Hume was a Benedictine monk...

Being nominated and then selected for senior roles within the Church falls largely on the Pope's representative in each country, although the decisions are taken in Rome. At the time of Cardinal Heenan's death, the Apostolic Delegate (or Papal Representative) in London was Archbishop Bruno Heim – who would, in 1982 in honour of Pope John Paul II's visit to Britain, become the first Ambassador (Nuncio) of the Vatican to the Court of St James since the Tudors.

Bruno was a great admirer of the English aristocracy and had already privately stated his own preference to have an English head of the Catholic Church of England. He was a gregarious fellow and a noted gourmet, with a great love of cooking, who liked to entertain his many friends at home in the Vatican Embassy in Parkside, Wimbledon. One close friend was the Queen Mother, for whom he would frequently cook, and he enjoyed many glasses of gin and tonic with her; she in turn entertained Bruno at Clarence House.

The process of electing a new Bishop is necessarily extensive and understandably lengthy, starts at diocesan level and works its way to the Congregation for Bishops in Rome.

Their vote on the best candidate is relayed by the Prefect of the Congregation for Bishops to the Pope, and the Holy Father will then make his decision.

So when the word came from Rome that the process for the successor of Heenan was not complete, a mystified Bruno asked, 'But what about Worlock? He is already lined up.'

'That's off,' he was told. 'Find out everything you can about this man Basil Hume at Ampleforth.' Bruno immediately dispatched a priest-diplomat from the Vatican Embassy, called Giovanni Tonucci, to Yorkshire. He was pretending to be at the Abbey on retreat, but was there to get to know Hume. According to Peter Bander van Duren, a writer on heraldry and a close friend of Nuncio Heim, Tonucci never managed to speak with the Abbot face-to-face but was able to scramble together a fairly detailed report on the unknown, and at that point, unknowing candidate.

Meanwhile Miles, supported by the two other members of his secret 'Back Hume' consortium – Norman St John Stevas, then Shadow Spokesman for Education and the Arts, and William Rees-Mogg, then influential editor of *The Times,* bombarded the Vatican and Bruno with instructions. The message was constant and clear: 'Hume is your man'. While popes have defied kings before now, it would take a brave man to deliberately go against the redoubtable Earl Marshall of England and his formidable cohorts. In the end, Pope Paul VI was like-minded, and Heenan's successor was announced in January 1976: Basil Hume.

It came as a tremendous shock to virtually everyone, that a little known monk had been chosen over the heads of several archbishops and numerous bishops and auxiliary bishops, to be the ninth Archbishop of Westminster – the biggest shock of all being to the Abbot himself. Indeed, when Bruno first consulted him by telephone at Ampleforth, monastic gossip has it that he believed someone was playing a trick on him.

It is customary for a nominee to be approached in advance and asked if he would accept the proposal. It was the traditional way of making sure there would be no embarrassing situations – though, of course, the nominee did not really have a choice, notably Hume, who was a monk under vows. When Bruno telephoned Hume, the Abbot was in his study.

'This is Bruno Heim, the Papal Nuncio,' he began. 'The Holy Father is proposing you as the new Archbishop of Westminster.' Hume sounded really annoyed, and snapped at Bruno, 'I will find out which House you are in and talk to your Housemaster about this stupid phone call.' He thought it was a teenage boy having a joke, and slammed the receiver down. Bruno asked his secretary, 'Are you sure this is the right number? I got a very peculiar man on the line who told me off.'

The second time Bruno called, Hume was even angrier. 'Stop this nonsense at once,' he bellowed. 'I can assure you this is not funny and your Housemaster will take an especially dim view of it.' Again, he slammed the receiver down.

The third time Bruno didn't give him a chance to speak. 'I am Bruno Heim and I'm coming for lunch and will be with you tomorrow.' Then he rang off himself.

That is how a very surprised, and embarrassed, Basil Hume learned he was being invited to leave his beloved monastery and school and become the next Archbishop of Westminster. The final confirmation of his new appointment was given to Hume while he was staying as a guest of the Queen at Windsor Castle. Known only to a few is the fact that on occasions, when she is in London, the Queen has what is called 'a grand bed and breakfast' at Windsor Castle, when she personally invites people she finds of interest for the weekend, who stay for dinner and breakfast.

Basil Hume was one of her guests at Windsor when the historic news was telephoned through to him by Bruno Heim:

'You *are* the Archbishop of Westminster.'

When the news was released to the public in January, Hume travelled up to London by car from Yorkshire and was deposited one evening on the steps of his new home, Archbishop's House, adjoining the Cathedral, wearing old clothes and carrying two battered suitcases containing his monk's habit and all his worldly possessions. Visitors were not usually expected at that time in the evening and it took Mr Murphy, the doorman, several minutes to reach the front door. He asked Hume what it was he wanted and was told, 'I'm to be your new Archbishop.'

To Mr Murphy, who was, by nature, even in the most normal circumstances, a suspicious man, an inspection of the tall, scarecrow-like figure – who was not even wearing a dog collar – and who was alien to any of Mr Murphy's preconceived images of his new boss, proved unconvincing. He was used to Cardinal Heenan, who was extremely formal and who would always be in clerical dress.

He told Basil Hume: 'You don't look like any archbishop I've ever seen.'

Hume said that it was only after several severe grillings that he was finally welcomed and ushered through the internal back door into his new residence. Though the unrepentant Mr Murphy said afterwards, according to some accounts, 'He still didn't look like an archbishop to me.'

Two months later, on the eve of his enthronement, poor Basil was to hear the same sentiment expressed by a London 'bobby' after going for a late night stroll and returning to find himself locked out of Archbishop's House. After supper, he had gone out in his ordinary clothes, he told me, and without a front door key, not realizing, as yet, that his staff and Mr Murphy, who lived in a separate building, all went to bed early.

'I rang the bell and hammered on the front door for ages,' he said, 'and when nobody came I became quite concerned, in view of what was to take place the next day – and thought I had better find an alternative way in.'

His best move would have been to walk around to the front of the Cathedral and enter through the main doors where people were still preparing for his big ceremony. Instead, he was caught trying to climb over the Choir School fence by a uniformed police officer, who was part of the advanced security team patrolling the Cathedral perimeter. Many Church leaders, politicians and celebrities would be attending the service and there was a high security alert, as this was also the period of intense IRA activity.

'He asked me what I was doing,' said Hume, 'and I told him I was the new Archbishop of Westminster trying to get into my home; that I had forgotten my key and didn't remember the telephone number.' He added, 'The policeman looked at me a bit oddly and said he thought I had better go with him, and I was marched to Rochester Road police station around the corner.' At the time there was a hospital nearby for the mentally ill, some of whom are allowed out into the community, among them being the odd one or two suffering from religious mania. 'I think the policeman believed I was one of those,' Hume told me.

The Cardinal said they were very polite to him in the police station and asked him where he was from. 'I've come from Yorkshire to be the Archbishop,' he told them. The police could get no answer when they tried to telephone Archbishop's House and Clergy House for confirmation. Eventually the police managed to locate someone in the Cathedral who knew the new Archbishop sufficiently well to identify him on the telephone. It turned out to be a monk who had travelled with his abbot to be with Hume in London. 'Oh yes,' he told the police, 'that is the Archbishop alright,' and Hume was escorted home where he was finally readmitted.

The next day, he told me, when he was in his full regalia, he saw the policeman who had collared him, and nodded to him. 'He looked embarrassed,' Hume said, 'though I must admit I was a much more recognizable figure with my mitre and crozier than the man caught after dark, clambering over the fence leading to a children's dormitory...'

Basil Hume's appointment was a huge personal and unwanted upheaval for him, and was an equally disturbing event in the diocese and in the country, for he was not universally popular among the secular clergy. As a monk he was not considered one of their own.

His predecessors, since the restoration of the Hierarchy (Dioceses and Bishops) of the Catholic Church in England in 1850, had all been bishops before being elevated to the 'top job'. As a monk, he had enjoyed a much freer way of life, albeit now considered unrealistic to a secular society. He owned nothing, had taken a vow of poverty and was, perhaps, a little out of touch with the outside world – except for an enthusiastic support for his beloved football team, Newcastle. It was hard for many of the clergy to understand him, and some of them never adapted, and refused to accept him. He won most of them over by his kindness and his ability to listen; one-on-one he was at his best.

But the shock of his appointment was a huge disappointment for those progressive conservatives who had been anticipating Derek Worlock's enthronement with pleasure. I don't believe Derek Worlock was very happy about it either – though he was made Archbishop of Liverpool as a consolation prize (it was where Heenan had been before becoming Archbishop of

Westminster). In Liverpool, Worlock found his niche. In a twenty-year partnership with Anglican Bishop David Shepherd and supported by ecumenical stalwart, The Methodist Chairman of Liverpool, the Reverend Dr John Newton, he tackled the social problems which emerged in the Thatcher era with huge success, bringing much needed understanding between the city's Catholics and Protestants.

Worlock was also the man who inspired and encouraged Bishop Vincent Nichols, a priest of the Archdiocese of Liverpool, appointed by the Pope in April 2009 as the new Archbishop of Westminster – the same Vincent Nichols who was the favoured protégé of Cardinal Hume, who pushed for him to be his successor at Westminster after he died... Good that these two men, once perceived as rivals and never exactly on friendly terms, should both have recognized Vincent's talent and marked him as a future leader of the Church.

Hume's style as Archbishop was not that of his predecessor, and was much more in the mould of an abbot. From the beginning Hume appeared to treat all the diocesan clergy like monks, because for all his life until then he had been dealing with monks. He treated them as though they were in vows, which they were not. His was not a democratic regime. As Abbot he had been used to giving orders and he chose not to alter his style when he changed his job. He was not one to debate a subject in advance of giving instructions, or consult committees; he often pretended to listen but didn't, and in the end he simply told people what to do. But these men had made no vows. When they were ordained as priests they had simply 'promised' to be obedient to their bishop. And that was it.

Monks and friars like myself take vows of poverty, chastity and obedience, in the same way as nuns. Secular priests do not vow celibacy. The Pope could change the ruling on marriage and they could then all marry if they wished, but the monks and friars and nuns can never marry, no matter what changes are made in the Church's rules, because they have all made vows, and are married to God. Many wear rings to show it – on the traditional wedding finger.

For a monk or friar his vows are ultimately more important than his priesthood. St Benedict and St Francis of Assisi were never priests – and it is also the case today for many monks and friars not to be ordained as priests.

What is more, Hume had a quite formidable stubborn streak. Until those in Westminster grew more accustomed to his style, even the bishops were wary of their new leader. To say his methods were occasionally a trifle unorthodox was perhaps dramatically understating the case! On one occasion in those early days, the Cardinal had invited a group of his bishops to Archbishop's House, to confer with him on a current problem in the Church.

They were unable to agree a solution so Hume produced a Frisbee and herded them all down to the Choir School playground where he made them take part in throwing and catching it. It helped focus their minds, he said, but some of them were shocked and concerned. The concept of the head of the Catholic Church in Britain getting his bishops to play a kids' game in their full robes would have been unthinkable under Heenan. And not to have taken part would have been unthinkable for Hume's bishops ...

Hume was, in fact, simply carrying out the admonition of Pope Paul VI, at their meeting in Rome just before his Enthronement, on March 25th 1976: 'Always remain a monk,' the pontiff said, meaning, 'Be yourself'.

I believe he probably inherited some of his stubbornness from his French mother, Lady Hume, who moved into Archbishop's House shortly after he became Archbishop – and became a holy terror. I doubt any archbishop in history before has had his mother move in to live with him. She was a most formidable woman and would constantly interfere with people who were waiting to see him. She would cross-examine them minutely about their business with her son and then tell the Cardinal, in strident tones, what she thought he should do. Eventually she became very ill and was moved into a Holland Park nursing home, run by nuns, where she subsequently died.

Basil proved from the start to be a hands-on leader. If he devised a plan, then he insisted on getting involved in its execution, and this proved invaluable, as few people were able to refuse him to his face. For example, the Cathedral Choir School finances were in a ghastly mess when he arrived.

Together with the Duke of Norfolk, he launched an appeal to preserve the Cathedral's world-renowned choir and school. He found solace and harmony in the Choir School, which echoed memories of his time as a teacher at Ampleforth. Most of his life had been spent in that environment and he would often join in the children's games – especially if it was soccer – and rarely missed any of the school's gala and sports days or prize-giving ceremonies. He had made saving the school his top priority. One of the things he determined to change was that a lay head teacher should be appointed – until then, the school had been run by a priest. The Cardinal personally tracked down a wonderful chap called Peter Hannigan who became the Choir School's first lay headmaster and made it the great success it is today, three headmasters on.

He tried to attend all the school's festive events and one Halloween night had promised to be at the children's fancy dress party as a judge, but was delayed. Derek Worlock, then Archbishop of Liverpool, was with the Cardinal in his study and their meeting was running very late. Eventually the children begged two of the priests, who were already in fancy dress, to go and fetch the Cardinal so the fun could start. One of these priests was dressed as a pirate and the other, Father Murphy (an extremely rotund, popular and fey cleric known as Murph the Smurf), was dressed as Miss Piggy.

The priests ran into the Cardinal's study and told him, 'The children have sent us to escort you down.' Miss Piggy then lisped 'Right now,' whilst curtseying. Worlock, who seemed devoid, in that moment, of any glimmer of humour, was outraged.

'What do you mean by this?' he spluttered.

'It means I have to go,' laughed Hume, 'and so do you!'

I suppose my being a friar and he a monk provided some form of understanding between us from the start, and over the years a strong bond developed between us.

I was extremely privileged to share in some of his more intimate moments. He was a remarkably shy and modest man who rarely revealed his inner feelings. He was a great champion of the poor even though he came from a reasonably well-off family and his politics leaned towards elements of the beliefs of both Tony Benn and his good friend Lord Longford. He adored simplicity and loathed ostentation of any kind, much preferring to wear casual ordinary clothes to being adorned in his cardinal's robes. Sometimes he would sit around in just his vest and without his socks and shoes.

He also had an eccentric sense of humour and an amazing ability to switch, in an instant, into three different characters who I called 'his people'. There was the drunken Irishman, done with a perfect Belfast accent, the drunken Scotsman (his father was a *borderer* and the Cardinal could perfectly mimic his accent), and the drunken Geordie, with the strong native accent of his home town of Newcastle.

Sometimes all three of his 'people' would appear in a single session. Each had a character of his own and was totally different to that of the Cardinal himself. He had all the slang associated with each one, down to a T and was a far better mimic than his good friend Rory Bremner.

He used his 'people' to voice beliefs he couldn't express as a cardinal, or to send up the Catholics. In his drunken Irish voice he would say: 'Ah, you've been messing around with those mealy-mouthed Protestants again, have you?' It was his way of signalling his approval, for whatever the funny voices said, Hume, of course, always meant the complete opposite. You could never keep up with him.

Or, when he was exasperated with a situation he might remark: 'Let's have a drink of whisky, that'll solve the problem,' in his drunken Scottish accent.

I first learned of his 'people' when he appointed me as his

Ecumenical Adviser on January 1st 1988. Ecumenical means encouraging universal Christian unity and bringing the faiths closer together, and he knew of my contacts with the Anglicans and Methodists and with Westminster Abbey.

'You seem to be taking these things seriously,' he said, then suddenly switched into his drunken Irishman: 'Someone's got to look after these troublesome Protestants, Michael, so it might as well be you.'

I was shocked until I spotted the twinkle in his eyes and realized that it was his oddball way of giving me his benediction for my role ahead. This, I learned, was one of the Cardinal's most important objectives during his term as Archbishop of Westminster, and one that endeared him to Catholics, Anglicans, Muslims and Jews alike. He was the person most responsible for creating an active spiritual dialogue between the faiths and did much to end the prejudices which then still existed in Britain against all Catholics.

His passion for Christian unity was unfortunately matched by his dislike for a number of the then Government's policies. He especially hated the Poll Tax and blamed Prime Minister Margaret Thatcher.

'The lady never bothers to listen to me,' he would complain after each meeting with the Blessed Margaret. 'I try to explain my serious concerns and she just pats me on the arm and says "Quite, quite" or "of course my dear" and I know she hasn't listened to a word I've said.'

Occasionally, when we drove past the entrance to Downing Street the Cardinal would lower his window and shake his fist and, in his drunken Geordie voice, say, 'Maggie out! Maggie out!' Not him saying it, of course, just the voice of some of the Blessed Margaret's subjects and Poll Tax rioters. But he was crafty using one of his 'people' to express the feelings of the ordinary working man. We both knew that the sentiment was also his own.

One day, after Margaret Thatcher was ousted, we were driving down Whitehall and passing the end of Downing Street, when sure enough, down went the window and up came the shaking fist and the cry of the drunken Geordie: 'Maggie out! Maggie out!'

'Calm yourself,' I told him, 'she's gone.'

'But I just like saying it,' he grinned back.

'But it's John Major now.'

'Alright,' he said, and changed the call: 'Major out! Major out!'

I, and I know of others too, have told the Cardinal's official biographers of his 'people' and some of his strange but endearing ways, but they have chosen not to record them. Yet this is the way he really was, and I hope that my anecdotes about the Cardinal will help people see him as a more human person with ordinary human frailties. And I hope to show him with qualities that will give him eventual formal public sanctity.

His political bias sometimes badly influenced the supposedly impartial role he was expected to play in British politics. In 1996, the Catholic Bishops of England and Wales prepared a statement called *The Common Good* which outlined the Catholic Church's social teaching. Hume had reluctantly presided over the development of the policy document at the Catholic Bishops' Conference that year, and had subsequently written the foreword. It was distributed just before the 1997 General Election.

Some people believed that much of the text therein derived directly from the Labour Party manifesto and that some kind of a 'behind the scenes' marriage was taking place between New Labour and the Catholic Church. Ann Widdecombe, in particular, claimed the document's partisan bias was dreadful and harangued me about the Cardinal's supposedly unfair support of her rival party's cause. After careful thought and prayer, I felt it was right for me to broach the subject with the Cardinal.

'Father, Ann Widdecombe is claiming you have told the Catholic Church to vote New Labour.'

'No, Michael, I have not told them that,' he replied, looking at me directly.

'Well she believes that is what *The Common Good* is saying – that various bits and pieces from the Labour Party manifesto are directly incorporated into it. Can I suggest Father that she may not be alone in this belief, and that I predict one of the newspapers, probably *The Guardian*, will pick up on this, and will print your photograph and say that you, or the Catholic Church, is endorsing New Labour.'

The Cardinal pointed to the door and shouted: 'Get out. Get out,' in his Geordie accent.

This was a routine we often went through and had always been meant in fun. He would tell me to get out and I would say 'Have you got a minute?' and he would say: 'I'm counting. One, two, three....' And I would often stay talking for up to an hour.

But this time there was no doubt in my mind he meant it. He was genuinely angry, and I left immediately.

In hindsight, while I believe he wanted to champion Catholic social teaching, he could see the difficulty of timing that the publication could possibly cause. In the event, the next morning my prediction was largely fulfilled when *The Guardian* carried an article worded almost exactly as I had suggested to him. I went directly to his office, where the door was always open, and placed the newspaper on the desk in front of him.

'There it is,' I said.

'You put it there,' was his reply.

'No I did not put it there! It was obvious to me as it was to anyone that some newspaper was bound to do it.'

'Then you're a witch!' was his intemperate response.

'I'm not a witch – or even a warlock,' I replied.

'It's not true anyway,' he said defiantly.

'I think you ought to go to confession,' I told him.

A little while later, while I was still in his office, he received a telephone call from Ann Widdecombe and I was somewhat shocked to hear him say, 'Yes, Miss Widdecombe.' It meant that he was still very angry. They were friends and he had always called her Ann until that moment. Ann told me afterwards that she had told him off, very nicely but very firmly and I guess the Cardinal's response meant that he was still a little angry about *The Guardian* piece.

Sadly, and too late to apologize, I had, like many others, unfairly judged him. I recently learned from an impeccable source that Cardinal Hume did, in fact, try to stop the publication of *The Common Good* not because he disapproved of the content of the social teaching but because its presentation and timing focussed attention away from where it should have been in his view. One can only hope that the forthcoming publication, *Common Good Two*, would be more attuned to the sensitivities of the late Cardinal...

Six months later, to everyone's relief, all seemed to have been forgiven between the Cardinal and Ann and he attended her fiftieth birthday party, held in the Churchill Room. We walked there together from the Cathedral and when we arrived Ann insisted that he sit next to her. He had recently fallen down the stairs in Archbishop's House and his arm was in a sling as a result, so because he could only use a fork, Ann cut up all his meat into tiny pieces. Hume had said Grace and gave a short speech in praise of 'my good friend, Ann', and I was overjoyed that these two dearly loved people were once more good friends with each other. There was one hilarious moment at the party, just before the entry of the birthday cake, when the lights were turned off and someone shouted 'Michael Howard must be coming'. The cake was carried in to the accompaniment of a gale of laughter.

Ann's and the Cardinal's great affection for one another was frequently expressed by both of them, but was markedly apparent on the occasion they exchanged special gifts. It came about because of a painting which I had been given.

It was a portrait of a cardinal in his scarlet robes and with white hair, fast asleep in his chair. His head is slumped forward and the book he has been reading is on the floor. In the foreground of the picture is a young Franciscan friar painting him. The artist is scratching his head, not knowing what to do, because the cardinal is fast asleep. The portrait's subject looked just like Hume, who also used to fall asleep in his chair every afternoon.

It was at a time when he was having his portrait painted by the famous artist Michael Noakes. One day, when the portrait was almost finished, I removed the real painting (which had been covered by some fabric) from its easel and replaced it with my own. I left the shroud off and turned the easel so the Cardinal would see it when he entered the room. He was reportedly quite shocked when he initially saw the painting but eventually discovered it was a joke and had been placed there by me. I was summoned to his study.

'Very funny Michael,' he said, adding, 'I would like that painting, I just love it.'

'Well I love it too and it's very precious to me so you can't have it,' I told him. 'You are having your own painted.'

'But I like that one,' he retorted. 'It is so naughty.'

When I told Ann, who also adored the painting and wanted it, she asked me if she could borrow the original for a few days so she could have two copies made, one for herself and one for the Cardinal. She signed one to him and he signed the other to her.

The Cardinal always liked to know what was going on with the people around him and loved to gossip. Sometimes we would sit and chat for hours. He often referred to me as his Miss Marple. He adored Agatha Christie's elderly sleuth and believed, like her, I was capable of uncovering the facts behind anything that was going on in and around the Cathedral. He knew I wouldn't tell him everything, because for various reasons it could have upset him or hurt him. But if at all possible, he liked to be *au fait* with what was going on. The best time to catch him would be at a quarter to the hour, for if he did have an appointment he would always try to ensure his visitors were gone by that time.

Cardinal Hume was a very saintly person but he did suffer

from mood swings and could have a mercurial temper and, for some reason, I would often be on the receiving end of his anger, never more so than in the days leading up to the memorial service for author Graham Greene in the Cathedral. On this occasion, it began with a provocative diary item in the Peterborough Column of *The Daily Telegraph*. The headline read 'No red hat for doubting Thomas', and speculated that Cardinal Hume would not be present at Greene's memorial service. Hume was still uncertain, at that time, just two days before the service, whether he should attend or not.

He was being difficult about it and we could not get a decision out of him, one way or the other, not that he had anything personal against Graham Greene. At the time of Greene's memorial, the Cardinal had been Archbishop of Westminster for fifteen years, and perhaps the, 'This is another one of those' syndrome might also have set in. Because he had been celebrant at the memorials for so many people, including Eamonn Andrews and Malcolm Muggeridge – who was incidentally a great friend of Graham Greene. He had put his heart into these, but it was plain to me he was becoming progressively more opposed to the burgeoning cult of celebrity.

He wasn't a puritan by any means, but he was wary of extravagant plaudits.

The 'doubting Thomas' phrase in the *Telegraph* headline referred to the name Thomas, which Greene had taken at his confirmation on becoming a Catholic when he was a twenty-one-year-old Oxford undergraduate. His religious conversion was we understand inspired not by faith alone, but also by his love for Vivien, another Catholic convert, who was to become his wife a year later. Greene left her after twenty years although they remained married for sixty-seven years until his death. Vivien would be present at his memorial, as would his companion of many years, Yvonne Cloetta.

I could understand the private convictions that made Hume reluctant to become involved and knew, just from his comments, that he didn't really want to participate, but it was infuriating not being able to get a decision out of him, one way or the other. Obviously Greene's relatives, particularly his son Francis, were anxious to know who would be the celebrant of the memorial service, not least because of the need to have the Order of Service printed.

The *Telegraph* piece, if nothing else, certainly stirred things up. It caused consternation among the family and clergy alike and alerted everyone to the Cardinal's dilemma. And this made him angrier than I had ever seen him. He always liked to blame someone when he was upset – and that someone usually turned out to be me. He would write 'Blame MS' in his diary in large letters if there was an appointment he didn't want to keep.

Petulant and schoolboyish? Yes. Frustrating? More so. But it was all part of the multifaceted experience of being close to this complex and devout man, who many were calling a living saint. That was Basil Hume. Almost childish in his simplicity – yet with an ethereal quality which made him spiritually radiant. I sometimes came close to throwing things at him and he stretched my patience beyond any limit – but in the end I forgave him everything. For I truly believe he was a man touched by God. Also, I admit, because he was so forgiving with me.

Not on this particular day though. This morning was to be a

Blame MS moment. We met in the lobby of Archbishop's House and the Cardinal strode over to me brandishing a copy of the *Daily Telegraph* and shouting, 'It's all your fault! I know it.'

'That's total nonsense', I told him. I was rather taken aback though decided – perhaps foolishly – to express some sympathy with the piece, since the Cardinal's procrastination was understandably upsetting the family.

He started to utter another accusation and I interrupted.

'Listen to me! If we are to discuss this, we are not doing so out here,' I told him and opened the door to a giant safe on the side of the lobby, which was being used to store paper and pens and other stationery, and hustled him inside, turning on the light and slamming the enormous door behind us. It was soundproof, ideal for the kind of heated discussion we were having. In retrospect, I admit it may seem more like a scene from a religious TV sitcom – the cardinal and the priest shut in a giant safe having a row – though in the reality version, thank God, the door did not lock behind us, as would inevitably have happened in a TV comedy. At least it stopped our comments reaching the Cathedral gossip machine.

I asked him, 'What are you going to do? Are you going to attend? Are you going to be the celebrant? Are you going to do anything at all?'

The Cardinal rather shyly replied, 'I don't know; I feel pushed into this.'

Seeking to understand the Cardinal's personal dilemma, I carried on. 'Listen, Father, while this has nothing to do with me directly, perhaps you are overreacting? You really do need to make a decision – are you going to attend or not?'

All the Cardinal felt able to reply, rather feebly, was, 'I don't know.'

Emboldened by my having secured the Cardinal in the safe, I continued: 'OK! We'll have to assume not. In which case, as we have only two days left, who do you suggest we ask to be celebrant and who should preach? Graham Greene has had the Order of Merit, so members of the Royal Family will be represented at the service. In honesty, Father, your indecision is making us look like country bumpkins.'

The irritation of the Cardinal seemed to have subsided somewhat and, by the look of him, he seemed to have recognized the seriousness of the situation. He asked what I would suggest. I replied that 'PoD was our man' – PoD was the affectionate nickname for Monsignor Patrick O'Donoghue, the then Cathedral Administrator (who has recently retired as Bishop of Lancaster). After a period of thought, the Cardinal gently nodded in agreement.

My biggest remaining concern was who should preach and whether this person could be available at such short notice; after all, not many would have been sufficiently knowledgeable about the author to preach a fine enough sermon. That aside, what I really wanted to say was that the Cardinal should preach. If Hume did the sermon, no-one would really care what he actually said; his presence and his aura would be enough. But in the circumstances, that was obviously out of the question. In the end, I suggested Father Roderick Strange, then Chaplain of the University of Oxford – now Rector of the Pontifical Beda College in Rome. 'Greene was at Oxford when he became interested in our Church,' I continued, 'so it is very appropriate.'

Hume pondered my suggestion for a few moments then nodded again. 'I agree. You must get in touch straight away.' I breathed a happy sigh of relief: the Cardinal had returned to his normal placid self. Amazingly, given the short notice, Father Roderick was delighted to be our preacher and promised he would be with us the following day. As for the Cardinal he still wouldn't decide if he was coming...

On the day itself, the Cathedral was packed with theatre and literary notables and the main eulogy was given by the late Sir Alec Guinness. I was seated on the sanctuary with the man I called 'Don Quixote', the remarkable Spanish priest on whom Graham Greene had based *Monsignor Quixote*, the central character in one of his last books. It was just before the service was due to commence that I spotted Hume, wearing his monk's habit, slip in largely unnoticed from the back of the sanctuary into the Canons' Stalls when everyone else was already in place. He took no active part in the service itself, and when the Mass had ended and the great procession had wended its way out, he slipped out the same way he had entered. He did not meet or greet anyone and one would scarcely have noticed him apart from his white hair.

There was one other odd moment during the service for the man who called himself a Catholic agnostic. One of the Cathedral's 'sacred college of oddities', the wonderfully odd and eccentric – though often holy – people, emerged from the shadows of the confessionals just as Alex Guinness began his eulogy.

She was wearing a pair of wellington boots, a plastic mackintosh and a sou'wester and carrying a newspaper. She proceeded across the front of the sanctuary to a vacant chair next to a surprised Lord Carrington (who was there representing Her Majesty) and made herself comfortable. The woman unfolded her newspaper, held it up in front of her, and proceeded to read – ignoring Alec Guinness just a few feet away. The great actor seemed mesmerized by her and stared at the lady fixedly while he gave his eulogy. No-one wanted to move in and create a scene by throwing her out but eventually she solved the problem herself by folding her newspaper, getting up and wandering out of the building, obviously bored by the speaker...

Over the years with Cardinal Hume, the unusual became the commonplace and I gradually learned to understand, and even anticipate, some of his somewhat eccentric behaviour. But he could still surprise me. One such night being in September 1991 when he was due to visit the former church of St John's Smith Square near Parliament. He had been invited to a concert and again it was one of those events where he had marked in his diary 'Blame MS'. The diary notation was just days old, although the invitation to this event, an ecumenical concert at which an American choir called *Gloriæ Dei Cantores* would be performing, had been extended and accepted months before. But now it clashed with a football match he wanted to watch and it was only after much grumbling and foot-stamping that he reluctantly agreed to go. Such behaviour was not meant to be taken seriously; it was his way of coping with frustration. He knew, and I knew, that without a genuine excuse he could not cancel any of these long-arranged appointments at the last minute.

After the concert, there was to be a reception in the crypt of St John's. The Bishop of London and several other religious leaders were there and wanted to meet him, but the Cardinal had become agitated and kept looking at his watch. I had introduced him to the conductor and turned away for just a moment to speak to someone else and in that instant he managed to disappear.

I learned over the years to recognize the Cardinal's genius as an escape artist. He could, like Houdini, find a way out of any enclosed space, and make his escape with no-one having seen him go. It took me nearly half an hour to discover that he hadn't just wandered off but had actually left the building. I only found out later that he had escaped through one of the fire exits with his then Private Secretary, Father Vincent Brady, to watch the second half of his football match...

Hume was a great admirer of the Methodists. He found them very holy and spiritual and non-institutional and became the Vice-President of Wesley's Chapel in City Road, the 'mother church' of Methodism, and where John Wesley is buried. He held a reception for the Methodists in Archbishop's House once a year and loved to support their big events. In 1997 he had agreed to preach at a special service at which the whole Methodist hierarchy would be present, as well as the senior representatives of the Catholic / Methodist Dialogue and the Methodist / Church of England Dialogue. I was very surprised he didn't cancel the engagement at the last minute because, as well as being in agony with a raging toothache, he was completely distraught over the sudden death of his great friend and press officer, Monsignor George Leonard. In the car he didn't say a word, just sat there in the front with his head bowed and occasionally groaning.

He had chosen to preach on the parable of the woman losing

a pearl of great value and then finding it again, but within moments of beginning he became hopelessly lost from his pre-prepared homily and started talking what might be termed 'scribble' – not making any sense at all. I looked around me to see how the rest of the congregation were taking it and found most of them staring up at the Cardinal in open-mouthed wonder and with reverence. I knew very well that his scrambled words were caused by the combined effects of his terrible grief and excruciating pain, but many present believed him to be 'talking in tongues', and the remainder concluded that it was a mystical happening. He was so revered by then that they readily accepted the nonsense he was speaking as a unique and awe-inspiring spiritual event. At the end of this speech, with the help of his Private Secretary, Father Jim Curry, I bundled him out even faster than he usually managed to escape by himself – before he gave the game away.

The Cardinal had a deep respect for women, young and old, and they for him, but he believed alter girls had no *fixed* place on the sanctuary. He was very traditional in this respect, and although he turned a blind eye to altar girls being used in some of the diocesan churches they were not at all welcome under his regime in Westminster Cathedral. Though things have changed in the past ten years. The majority are now girls!

One Holy Thursday, when a parish priest arrived to concelebrate the Chrism Mass, when all priests publicly renew their priesthood and loyalty to the bishop, he brought with him a whole gaggle of altar girls. Clearly no-one had warned the unfortunate cleric that his young entourage, however pretty and diligent they were in their duties, would find no favour with the Cardinal.

Hume was informed by his Master-of-Ceremonies that altar girls had been brought in to assist at the special Chrism Mass, at which it was the custom for all altar boys, adult altar servers and priests to attend. A priest was dispatched by Hume with the message, to the effect of: 'Get these girls off my sanctuary'.

The actual priest who had brought them was immediately protective of his charges. 'They are with me,' he said, as though this would automatically solve the problem.

'Then you'd better take them home now,' he was advised.

The priest took umbrage at this, and forming his score or more girls into two ranks, stormed out of the Cathedral with his girls marching behind him.

Apart from his beloved football, the Cardinal was not much of a television viewer. He did like the BBC series Dad's Army as well as the comedy sitcom *Keeping Up Appearances* and was an ardent fan of both the character Mrs Bucket and Patricia Routledge, the actress who played her. Hume said he thought one of his nuns, who lived in Archbishop's House and looked after him, was a perfect match for Mrs Bucket (the character insisted that the name was pronounced 'Bouquet').

Sister Mary Bernard was very dame-like, and ruled the house, the other nuns, the Cardinal and his Secretary, and stood no nonsense from any of them. Hume loved shepherd's pie and asked for it several times a week. But Sister Mary refused to make it. 'Far too difficult' she always told him. But he and I were always convinced this was simply a power move by Sister 'Bucket' to keep *common* dishes out of her house and keep up appearances. He secretly thought she was quite splendid, though he wasn't always comfortable with the women he encountered –

especially those women, like Jennifer Paterson, who were outspoken and outrageous.

Jennifer and I had met casually, in the street, in 1985. She was a loud, laughing cook, much loved in society despite her eccentricities, but known to the nation only in her last years, along with Clarissa Dickson Wright, as one half of the celebrated culinary duo, the Two Fat Ladies. Jennifer lived just across the road from the Cathedral with her saintly uncle, Anthony Bartlett who carried a cushion at Hume's funeral on which lay the Cardinal's medals.

With her flamboyant style, lavish layers of 'bling', painted nails, and incessant smoking while she cooked, Jennifer was a captivating focus for a modern TV audience. Both she and Clarissa were enormous, had wonderfully deep voices, and were incredibly grand and the most marvellous fun to be with. Jennifer, who was expelled from convent school for being disruptive, had become a deeply conservative Catholic who considered Cardinal Hume a progressive liberal. She disliked the Cathedral and worshipped regularly at the Brompton Oratory, where Mass is still said in Latin, and also in the Extraordinary Form, and attention is given to the more ancient ceremonies.

She was an absolute dervish on her motorbike, a TT-loving pensioner who roared through the congested streets of London with complete confidence until she was seventy. She carried me several times as a pillion passenger and I admit to being terrified the whole time, clinging onto her generous girth with both hands and travelling, mainly, with my eyes tight shut. It was said that she would ride home from boozy lunches – on one occasion, puzzled by the big roundabout at Shepherd's Bush, she rode up on to the grass for a better view.

Luckily she never killed anyone – though came close when, in a fit of pique, she hurled several dirty coffee mugs from the upstairs window of the offices of the *Spectator* (where she cooked the weekly *Spectator* lunch) which landed in the next door garden of the National Association of Funeral Directors.

Jennifer favoured vodka in the mornings, would lunch on pasta and red wine and would drink whisky thereafter. It was not unknown for her to become a little unpredictable as the evening wore on.

In this light, someone's judgment must have been on tilt, when whoever it was had invited her to an academic-cum-theological dinner at the House of Lords. It was a gathering to raise funds for the Lady Margaret Beaufort Institute of Theology in Cambridge. Lady Margaret was the mother of Henry VII and grandmother of Henry VIII, a noted intellectual and a very devout Catholic. I was attending with the Cardinal and was seated next to Jennifer.

The Institute, which specializes in theology, spirituality and leadership for lay ministry, was established in 1993 to combat prejudice and recognize the valuable contribution women have to offer. It was the first such Roman Catholic house of studies for women. Whoever invited Jennifer should have known that as a staunch Catholic conservative she might just take issue with the whole concept of women in the Church.

The Cardinal's eyes opened wide when he saw her because he also knew that she didn't really fit in there. Our eyes met and I shrugged, trying to indicate that her presence there had nothing to do with me. But he had probably noted it down somewhere as a 'Blame MS' situation. She was already making a fuss because she wanted whisky and the House of Lords serves only wine at a set-menu dinner. She wasn't at all happy, and when Jennifer wasn't happy she could make everyone else around her very unhappy. 'How am I expected to enjoy myself without a glass of whisky?' she complained. Knowing from experience that things could only get worse if she didn't have her way, I slipped out of the dining room and grabbed the first waiter I could find.

'This is an emergency', I told him. 'A lady is in desperate need. Please could you find me a bottle of whisky?' He was gratifyingly efficient and turned up at my side within five minutes with an unopened bottle. 'Like a gift from God,' beamed Jennifer, twisting off the cap and pouring an alarmingly generous measure into her glass.

'No. I actually got him to put it on your bill,' I told her, as she took a long swallow.

At that moment the Cardinal was called upon to say Grace and everyone fell silent. He said it in English but when he reached the part, 'In the name of the Father, and of the Son and of the Holy Spirit' Jennifer leapt to her feet, waving her glass and shouted, 'Ghost! Ghost! Not Spirit, Ghost!'

The Catholic Church previously prayed 'Ghost' but this had been changed to 'Spirit' in the sixties. As a traditionalist Catholic, Jennifer didn't approve of the change. The Cardinal was obviously angry at being heckled, but after a brief pause he continued with Grace and sat down, glaring in our direction. I pulled Jennifer down to her seat, but short of gagging her, I couldn't get her to stop complaining. She kept digging me in the ribs with her elbow, and there was nothing fat about that. It was quite hard, and painful for me.

'It should be Ghost,' she kept hissing in a stage whisper, a bit like a pantomime baddie. 'I think spirit is much more appropriate for you', I told her, nodding towards the rapidly emptying whisky bottle. But Jennifer wasn't done.

After another glass of her preferred poison, she once again jumped to her feet and bellowed in her deep voice, 'Why am I here? What am I doing here?'

'You're here aren't you? So you must have accepted the invitation,' I whispered, tugging at her skirt to make her sit down but she was having none of it. She pushed my hand away and continued, 'Who are all these women?' spreading her arms and indicating the other female guests. 'Women in the Church? I don't know if I like that. I don't know if I really want to see women involved in the Church.' I told her to calm down and have another drink and after glowering at everyone for a few moments longer, she sat down and reached for her glass.

In the end the people who had thrown us such disapproving looks, were glad she was there. Those who were in attendance, Cambridge chancellors, vice chancellors and professors and their special guests were being, may I say, a trifle prudent with their donations and it was Jennifer who harangued them into giving more. 'You should add plenty of noughts on your cheques,' she told them imperiously, repeating, 'I want to see lots of noughts.' And they responded.

Jennifer died in 1999 shortly after Cardinal Hume's demise. It is alleged that she asked for caviar as her last meal but expired before she could eat it. Her funeral was held in her beloved Brompton Oratory and her coffin was carried out with her motorcycle helmet sitting on top. What a lady!

One of the most seismic events of the last century in recent Church history was the decision by the Church of England on 11 November 1992 to ordain women to its priesthood. This led directly and indirectly to hundreds of clergy and thousands of laity mentally, if not physically, leaving the Church of England. For some it made the comparatively new Archbishop of Canterbury, George Carey, the most unpopular Church leader of his time; for others, an inspirational leader who championed progression. Dr Carey was left in a no-win situation, and I felt sorry for him.

The Catholic Church in England had been preparing for the possible moment of the ordination of women in the Church of England since I was appointed as Ecumenical Advisor to the late Cardinal in 1988, and in that position I found myself at the centre of events. The Cardinal and I met at 6.30am on the day of the vote to revise his final statement, which was sent to the Vatican to synchronize our response whichever way the vote went. If the move to ordain women failed, we would applaud a sensible conclusion and say how good it was that we could continue to share in common the nature of the priesthood. Alternatively we would say how saddened we were by the result and explain how difficult this was for uniting the two Churches.

It is estimated that eventually over a thousand men resigned their orders, of whom about a few hundred were married (the majority of those with children), and thousands of laity left the Anglican Church. The movement of such large numbers of Anglican clergy to the Catholic Church created a huge issue, but also a wonderful and blessed opportunity. Despite some notable outbursts – including from one Anglican vicar from Hull who brought a coffin to London labelled 'Church of England RIP' and organized a formal cortege through the capital and around the green of Westminster Abbey, before a 'funeral service' – I was too occupied with two thorny questions posed by the mass defection of Anglican priests to take much notice of these expressions of despair among the remaining clergy.

The problems the Church faced were serious ones: how to accommodate married men as Catholic priests and how to pay for it all? Most of the issues had been worked out in advance during countless meetings with Anglican clergy and senior lay people in Church House (the centre of 'political' life in the Anglican Church in England). We knew almost precisely what would happen if the vote went in favour of women priests and the Church of England leaders were very sensitive to the problems their defectors would face.

Most importantly, from the outset, Cardinal Hume championed the move to create married Catholic priests in England from those married clerics received from the Anglican Church. He was also very aware of the special doubts and concerns that their wives would have about a switch to Catholicism. He wanted them to feel comfortable if the change came and suggested we hold informal weekly meetings for the wives, over sandwiches and coffee, to give them a chance to voice their concerns. He sat casually among them in his armchair and personally answered all of their questions. The women came from all over the country to attend these informal get-togethers with the Cardinal, who told them, openly and honestly, that initially the Catholic parishioners might find it difficult to adapt. It would be somewhat traumatic for some of them to knock at a priest's door and have it opened by a small child who would shout 'Daddy' to summon the priest. The Cardinal wrote personally to every congregation in the country asking them to be welcoming and accepting of these married priests and their wives and children. In the end, parishioners readily accepted the newcomers and adapted easily.

The financial strain on both the Church of England and the Catholic Church was considerable: in the Anglican Church's provision, everyone with less than ten years' service received no 'redundancy payment' (which included every priest in his twenties); qualifiers received a fraction of their income as a payoff. It was tragic for many of those who chose to leave the Anglican Church over the issue, but who would not become Catholics, and many of those who obeyed their consciences lost everything, including their homes.

Eight days after the vote in 1992, I was invited to meet with Cardinal Ratzinger, who was then Prefect of the Congregation for the Doctrine of the Faith – originally known as the Holy Inquisition. His imposing headquarters in Rome were built at the same time as St Peter's and I was greeted there by my old friend, Monsignor Josef Clemens, who was at the time his Private Secretary, who took me to a room the size of the Buckingham Palace Throne Room, and asked me to wait. Moments later, Cardinal Ratzinger entered through a secret door disguised as part of the wallpaper, which one couldn't see until it was opened. His opening words to me were, 'Father Seed, you're very young.' I kissed his ring and replied, 'You don't look that old yourself!'

Rumour had it that he was an overly serious, dour old

hardliner but I found him to be neither. He really did look much younger than his years and he was both friendly and chatty and made me feel at ease. His English is perfect and he talked to me at length about his sister, who had just died, and his brother, Georg, a musician and priest in his home town. Cardinal Ratzinger is also a talented musician and pianist and is passionate about good choral music. He was inquisitive about my childhood and during the two hours we spent together most of it was taken up with family matters. Finally though he broached the subject of the 'converting' Anglican priests.

He said the Pope wanted to be most welcoming and fully endorsed Cardinal Hume's proposal of a special dispensation permitting married priests. He praised the Cardinal's role in the whole transitional process, and urged me to continue my work with Christian unity and in the helping of those in spiritual need. He urged for Cardinal Hume to be generous in his response.

Through his friends I later discovered Cardinal Ratzinger's love of the English ale Spitfire, brewed in Kent by Shepherd Neame, Britain's oldest family-owned brewer, and his collection of London beer mats and have, since our meeting, had both couriered to him on several occasions by visiting clergy. He is always enthusiastically appreciative they say, and I understand that his tastes have not changed. A rather ecumenical gesture from our wonderful German Pope.

After the vote in 1992, we were inundated with requests from would-be-converts and I suggested the Cardinal open his doors to them on Wednesday evenings. On the night of the first assembly I put out fifty chairs but over 250 Anglican deacons, priests and bishops turned up. Eventually some of them decided against becoming Catholic priests but many hundreds more were Received. One London parish, St Matthew's in Bethnal Green, where the Kray family had their funerals, the priest, curate and deacon all opted to be ordained into the Catholic Church along with almost the entire congregation. A Catholic bishop, Victor Guazzelli, went and received all of them into the Catholic Church in their own Anglican church. David Hope, then Bishop of London, had given his approval but not all the locals were happy about it and the few who did not want to 'convert' had to find a new church. They felt abandoned by their own Church and it caused a lot of tension. St Matthew's, although owned by the Church of England, had become a shared Anglican / Catholic Church overnight. The Catholic Church couldn't afford to buy it, so it was rented and this arrangement was made for two other churches in London which became – and remain – half-and-half, Catholic and Anglican.

The Church of England had had women readers and deaconesses and deacons since the seventies and many of these rushed to be ordained immediately after the vote. Women were presenting themselves from all walks of life for ordination. It is understood that many had not had time to think the whole process through too carefully.

Cardinal Hume had a favourite saying: 'Ordain in haste and repent at leisure.' Meaning if you ordain someone too quickly then you are stuck with them if you have made a mistake.

Personally I recognize the feminine contribution and that there are some extremely gifted women priests but I prefer to leave the question of their ordination to those better qualified to judge.

Hume would ridicule himself if asked if he approved of women priests, and say that he was not an 'impossibilist'. He did not particularly want the ordination of women, he said, but if it came he would accept it.

'There would be no problem if I could dismiss the first ten thousand applicants who offered themselves for the priesthood,' he stated. He had a wicked sense of humour and was very naughty, and meant that he wouldn't want a band of wild women ordained – he'd refuse all the bolshie ones.

Then he would add: 'But I am a man under authority,' meaning he was ruled by the Pope and the Church's teaching.

All I can say is 'Thank God' for the enormous bond between Basil Hume and his close friends, the Archbishops of Canterbury, Cogan, Runcie and Carey.

Earlier in this chapter I mentioned Parkside, the home of the Vatican Ambassador, which had been given to the Catholic Church by Sir Joseph Hood when the first Apostolic Delegate (or official papal representative) in Britain was appointed in 1938. His son Sir Harold Hood, who inherited the baronetcy shortly before his fifteenth birthday, had a brother called Robin.

One memorable occasion relating to Robin occurred during the annual reception hosted at Archbishop's House for distinguished Catholics in high office. They were dressed in their finery, including, where appropriate, chains of office.

I was present in my simple brown Friar's habit, when Robin Hood and his wife Miriam approached me. We were in deep conversation when I became aware of the presence of one of the assembled chained guests. I asked who he was and he announced, 'I am the Sheriff of Nottingham, and this is my wife.'

Well I was, to say the least, a little lost for words – I didn't dare look at Robin or his wife to see their reactions; Robin was not known for his enormous sense of humour. Deciding that my best course of action was simply to introduce the Sheriff to my previous interlocutors, I said, 'Well this is Robin Hood and his wife, Miriam.'

The Sherriff gave me a disparaging look and replied, sarcastically, 'And I guess that makes you Friar Tuck?'

I later learned that the Sherriff, in high dudgeon, had approached the Cardinal and exclaimed 'That man, over there', gesticulating in my direction, 'has sent me up. I am the Sheriff of Nottingham', he proudly announced, 'and this Friar said that he', now pointing in the direction of Robin, distinctive because of his rather vibrant 'blonde' wig (he was undergoing a course of chemotherapy at the time), 'is called Robin Hood. It is an outrage!'

The Cardinal, recognising the amusing confusion in the matter, could not conceal a smile, and replied simply, 'It is he'.

As in the tales of yore – exit one deflated Sherriff.

FIVE

A PUNK AT RECEPTION – HOW THE *MATCH OF THE DAY* THEME WAS SNEAKED INTO HUME'S FUNERAL – LUNCH WITH SNOOPY AND WOODSTOCK – MOTHER THERESA COMES A-CALLIN' – NARROWLY AVOIDING SQUASHING A FUTURE POPE – DIANA – 'ENJOY, BUT DON'T INHALE'

One day a young man, with spiky, punk-style, multicoloured hair appeared at Archbishop's House and announced that he was our new receptionist. He had been personally chosen, he said, by Cardinal Hume. He was about eighteen and answered to the name of Brian.

At that time we had two receptionists who were growing old in the job – the very proper and dignified Harry Murphy, a wonderful old Irishman, devoted to the Cardinal, but suspicious of everybody who came to Archbishop's House – who, with his late wife and children, had been there since the fifties – and David Fox, his equally delightful colleague, who was also a longtime retainer. The Cardinal considered Mr Murphy was of an age when he needed a little help and that's when Brian was taken on.

The Archbishop would regularly 'adopt' people, of all kinds, particularly young people. They would come and talk to him and be counselled by him, and he was able, through these chats, to keep in touch with the youth culture of the day, and, I think, be given a reminder of his years as a monk and teacher at Ampleforth Abbey and School.

Almost from the time he arrived at Westminster, Hume had invited these young people to come in and talk, and they clearly adored him, and felt privileged to belong to this very special and informal club he had going. He was helped and supported in this by his then Private Secretary, Father John Crowley.

I'm not sure just how Brian was opted onto the staff but he was introduced to the Cardinal by a later Private Secretary, the dynamic Canon Pat Browne. Hume never revealed why he chose Brian as a receptionist but he seemed perfectly comfortable with his new protégé's appearance – which was unconventional by Archbishop's House standards to say the least.

Brian's punk hair style caused many of the Cardinal's visitors' eyebrows to lift. He had little spikes of different colours, mainly blonde, but it was a changeable feast. Brian also wore a ring in his ear when he first arrived, though I think he had both ears and his nose pierced. He smartened up as time went by but at the outset one never saw him with a tie and he wore casual clothes. He had several rings on each hand and some letters tattooed on his fingers.

I think one of the nuns or Mr Murphy must have had a quiet word with him, for after a week or so he began appearing for duty in a conventional suit and tie – with only two finger rings and the one in his ear. But these were his only concessions to Archbishop's House solemnity – and he retained his own, very distinctive style of receiving visitors.

It didn't take long to discover what had brought about the bonding between Brian and His Eminence. They were both obsessed with soccer. Hume was born in Newcastle and from about the age of six or seven, went to all United's home, and many of its away, matches and he remained a dedicated and lifetime supporter of his home team, nicknamed 'The Magpies'. As a student at Ampleforth, he was captain of the rugby team and was also a keen cricketer, but his great passion was for soccer.

Brian was a supporter of a London team. Each was totally committed to his own team and this frequently led to heated arguments and much crowing and posturing and insult hurling. Some of this took place through the two-way intercom which connected the Cardinal's desk in his office on the first floor with the entry lodge downstairs. Archbishop's House has an incredibly grand staircase sweeping up to the first floor to an enormous room called the Throne Room. The Cardinal's office was close to this grand salon.

Sometimes when he was with a visitor – it could even be the Archbishop of Canterbury – Brian's voice, loud and unannounced, would come booming through the intercom. It was quite irrelevant to Brian that Hume might be in mid-conversation with someone important. Without any warning, the intercom would burst into life and Brian would start to harangue the Cardinal about Newcastle's performance in a game, or trumpet the success of his own team.

No matter how serious the conversation he was interrupting Brian would shout his news – often denigrating Hume's beloved Newcastle United, through the intercom. 'You lost. Your stupid team lost again! They're all rubbish,' would be a typical interjection. And the Cardinal would shout back, 'We're not as rubbishy as your team. Wait till you come up against us and we'll show you who's rubbish. Your lot should be kicked out of the league.'

The language could be even more saucy on Feast Days when the Cardinal would switch in an instant into one of the three different characters whom he called his 'people', favouring, for football comments the drunken Geordie, with the strong native accent of his home town Newcastle. Not him speaking, of course, but a drunken Geordie football supporter.

Argument over, he would then carry on the conversation with his jaw-dropped visitor as though nothing had happened. Some of the leading secular and religious leaders of the world have had their tête-à-têtes with the Cardinal interrupted in this way, and he never offered them a single word of explanation, or apology.

On one particular occasion, I remember the Cardinal was expecting the newly appointed Archbishop of Canterbury and Brian wasn't quite sure who he was. He was always polite but could be a little short with visitors. Many great personalities like the Dalai Lama, Mother Theresa, Billy Graham and heads of other churches and royalty were greeted by Brian, who knew few of them by sight, and treated everyone exactly the same. His role evolved to becoming more of a guardian of the Cardinal rather than a simple provider of access.

I had asked Brian to let me know when the Archbishop arrived and when I heard the front door bell sound while I was on the first floor and nobody then came up the stairs, I became curious and went down to investigate. There were two 'doorman's boxes', one on either side of the corridor just a few feet inside the main entrance. I found the then newly appointed Archbishop of Canterbury, George Carey, meekly sitting in dark shadows, on a small chair in the tiny cul-de-sac passage next to one of the boxes, looking concerned – almost disbelievingly – at Brian who was sitting opposite in the other box reading *The Sun* newspaper.

The Archbishop hadn't even made it to the foot of the grand staircase.

When I asked Brian what he was doing there he told me, 'I told this geezer I would see if the Cardinal was ready for him, but I haven't had a chance to call him yet.'

I said, 'Well please do it now Brian,' and I led the poor Archbishop up the stairs. Not a very graceful welcome for His Grace on that occasion, I'm afraid.

The Cardinal's love of soccer almost landed him in trouble with the law on more than one occasion. He was stopped several times by police for speeding, hurrying back from an appointment to watch *Match of the Day*, or some other football programme. Luckily for him, on each occasion, it was a sympathetic policeman who stopped him. Apart from having one of the best known faces in Britain, he was not that difficult to recognize in his scarlet robes. On one occasion he told me, 'Two of them turned out to be soccer fans and quite understood my need to rush back.'; on another, after he had been stopped when racing back from Ampleforth in Yorkshire, the police provided a motorcyclist to drive ahead of his car so he could go faster and make it home in time to watch the game.

The Cardinal had a little TV room where he watched football and would often have young people in with him to watch the games. All of them drinking cans of lager. Most of these youngsters had lost a father or mother, or both, and Hume was sitting in as a kind of uncle-cum-father figure. He was eventually given a video recorder and was able to record his favourite matches, but this hardly affected his desire to speed home. He preferred to watch the games live, he told me.

Hume had never wanted an official car and had ordered the sale of the previous Cardinal's car – a formal black limousine – when he arrived. He preferred an ordinary, modest four-door family saloon which was registered in the name of his priest Private Secretary. In this way any parking fines or speeding tickets would end up with the Secretary.

He would nearly always sit in the front. Being a tall man he was able to slide the front seat right back and could stretch out. It was tough on anyone seated behind him who had to squat with their knees under their chins. But that rarely happened, because he hated giving a lift to anyone. He would say 'my car is not a taxi', and he meant it!

Even people returning from the same place would be ordered to take a bus or walk. He usually said his 'Monastic Office', his set daily prayers for morning, evening and night, or slept on journeys and did not like to talk to people. He said that about the only time he had any privacy or time to himself was in the car, time for reading, praying or thinking. It was precious time alone, and he protected it jealously.

I would go with him sometimes, particularly to ecumenical and inter-faith events, and his priest secretary was usually with us, acting almost as a kind of gentleman in waiting. But Hume was satisfied that I knew his rules, which were short and simple:

'Shut up and be quiet'. I was told this at the start of every journey. With Hume in the front, people were often puzzled to see the man in the scarlet robes in the passenger seat and the one in the back wearing a simple dog collar.

Sometimes the Cardinal would procrastinate over signing certain documents and I developed a foolproof method of speeding the decision. I found that if I waited until half time during an important match, and took the papers into his television room, then I could almost certainly count on them being signed just so he could be rid of me before the second half started.

Whenever possible he would attend the Newcastle games in person. He would wear a black-and-white striped club scarf and hat and knew all the players personally, though he counted Kevin Keagan as an especially good friend. The Magpies were his pride and joy and he even kept his little round red cardinal caps – about five or six of them – on the head of a Newcastle United teddy bear in his office.

The Geordies were as devoted to Cardinal Hume as he was to his home town and they erected an enormous statue of him just outside the train station, which was unveiled by The Queen in Her Jubilee Year, 2002. The prankster in the Cardinal would have loved it when a Geordie streaker dashed in front of the Duke of Edinburgh and the Queen on the occasion of the unveiling.

Match of the Day was certainly among his favourite television programmes and he had actually appeared in their studio as a commentator on some of Newcastle United's matches. What is known to very few people is that he made a special request that the *Match of the Day* theme music should be played at the end of his Requiem Mass, as his coffin was being carried away in procession. Our Master of Music at the time, the brilliant James O'Donnell, cleverly interwove the theme into a classic organ solo and I suspect that few in the congregation noticed this final tribute to our soccer-mad Cardinal.

James was later head-hunted by Westminster Abbey and became the first Catholic Organist and Master of Choristers since the Reformation. And, in a bizarre switch, we replaced him with the equally brilliant Martin Baker, who had been the acting Master of Music at the Abbey.

Hume's diary was arranged up to two – even three - years in advance, and he was very aware of this. But he would become absolutely furious if one of his appointments clashed with an England or Newcastle game.

On one occasion we had to go, as guests of Sir Sigmund Sternberg, to address a Jewish-Christian dinner event at the Royal Overseas League. The Chief Rabbi was the other guest of honour. England was playing soccer that evening and I arrived in the Cardinal's office an hour before we were due to leave and found him stomping up and down with temper.

'I am very angry with you,' he snapped. 'How did this thing get put in the diary. This is appalling.'

He was aware that nobody could have possibly known at the time the appointment was agreed that England would be playing that night. But he was still furious.

'Why am I going?' he asked me.

'You have to go. That's your job. You're the Cardinal, and that's what Cardinals do. That's why you're here,' I told him.

He growled: 'I have to say something?'

'Why not just say bubblygum, bubblygum,' I said. 'It's just your presence, your aura, they want. It doesn't matter what you say. You're so loved by the country. You've reached a stage where you don't have to speak. You just have to be there.'

'Stop this nonsense,' he said, more gently. 'I have to say something.'

But he understood what I was saying. Towards the end it was his presence they wanted. And when he did speak it was never for more than about three minutes.

Cardinal Hume was one of the most unpredictable people I have ever known, with an infinite capacity to surprise. But even I was astonished the day he engaged a giant Snoopy in conversation over lunch. It was just like a rerun of that old movie *Harvey*, in which James Stewart plays Edward P Dowd – a man with a six-foot talking rabbit as a friend.

This crazy lunch took place in the Cardinal's formal dining room, a very grand affair with a twenty-foot long table sitting on a large, reddish Persian carpet, with giant candelabras and two spectacular chandeliers, and a big, open fireplace surmounted by a massive mirror and with an ornate old clock on the mantelpiece.

The man responsible for this bizarre lunch was Viscount Anthony – known as Tony – Furness, a truly eccentric, but lovable, sometime theatre producer who lived off the interest of a £50 million fortune.

His American mother, Thelma, a society beauty and bit-part film actress had a long and celebrated affair with Edward VIII, who became the Duke of Windsor after his abdication, and Tony was persistently rumoured to be the disgraced King's illegitimate son. It was Thelma, when she tired of him, who, at a party in her home, introduced Edward to Mrs Wallis Simpson, who caused the abdication crisis in 1936.

Tony and I became friends in the mid eighties, after meeting in the Cathedral during one of his visits to England. He was then living in America, where he had been brought up by his mother after she separated from the late Lord Furness. He later spent the last year of his life at the Hospital of the Order of Malta in London, from where he would make frequent sorties in a wheelchair, clad in a mink toque, leather motorcycle gauntlets, white scarf and Sherlock Holmes-style cape. He cut quite a dash as he was trundled through Knightsbridge and Mayfair.

He was a devout Catholic and a generous benefactor of the Cathedral – he was a Member of the Guild of St Gregory (for senior altar servers) – and The Passage, the centre for the homeless founded by Hume. I would often dine with him at the Stafford Hotel off St James's Street, which was his favourite. Tony suffered with a bad stutter and on occasions a conversation could last all night. He came across as being rather naive in his manner, though was a stickler for things being done correctly and carefully.

In 1987, he telephoned from America and said he would like to meet with the Cardinal to discuss a large donation he wished to make to the Church. Hume was delighted and invited him to come for lunch, but was surprised when Tony asked if he could bring a couple of friends with him. The Cardinal told him that was fine and looked forward to seeing the three of them. What a threesome. The two friends turned out to be giant-sized, stuffed versions of Snoopy and Woodstock. Tony had brought them from America on Concorde where they shared their own £7,000 seat; Woodstock had sat on Snoopy's lap for the journey, Tony told me.

He arrived at Archbishop's House with an assistant, carrying one of the huge cartoon characters under each arm. The nun who showed Tony and his assistant to the Cardinal's rooms was very flustered after being introduced to Snoopy, and her eyes were almost popping out when she reached the first floor. It was decided immediately to seat Snoopy and Woodstock at the dining table while Tony would await the Cardinal in his parlour. The assistant went on his way.

When Hume appeared, he shook hands with Tony and said, 'I thought you were bringing two friends with you. Are they not joining us?'

'They are already here,' Tony told him. 'They have gone through to the dining room. You will meet them there.'

'Wouldn't they like to join us for a drink before lunch?' asked Hume. 'I don't think so,' replied Tony.

The Cardinal, not wishing to keep them waiting, suggested his guest should go through to lunch. They walked to the dining room and there were Snoopy and Woodstock, life-sized, sitting at his table. Hume always sat at the head of the table and Snoopy had been placed on the side, to his left, with Tony facing the dog with Woodstock on his right.

'Please say hello to my friends,' said Tony, and Hume found himself shaking hands and wishing 'good day' to the two cartoon characters.

Hume could usually adapt to anything and it didn't seem to faze him in the slightest. He happily included Snoopy and

Woodstock in the conversation during lunch, asking how they had all met and if they were enjoying being together in London.

Before leaving Tony handed the Cardinal a generous cheque for the Cathedral and told him he had decided Snoopy was so happy in Archbishop's House he had decided to leave him there as the Cardinal's guest.

'Will you be able to take care of him?' he asked, and the Cardinal assured him that he would make sure Snoopy was well catered for.

Now there were not many areas in Archbishop's House where one could put a man-size cartoon dog without it seeming out of place, but the Cardinal finally decided to sit him in a chair on the stairs outside his bedroom. He said 'goodnight' to him each time he passed on his way to bed.

After some months had passed, Hume asked me if I thought the Westminster Children's Hospital in nearby Vincent Square, where I was Chaplain, would like to have the Snoopy. I told him I thought the children would love him and so I was tasked with carrying him around to the hospital where I presented him to a delighted Matron.

More months went by and Snoopy was forgotten by both of us until one day I was summoned urgently to the Cardinal's study.

He immediately demanded to know where 'that person' was.

I asked, 'Which person?'

'Where is he? He's not in the chair any more.'

I suddenly realized he was talking about the giant Snoopy. 'You told me to give him to the Children's Hospital.'

'Oh dear,' he said. 'You'll just have to get him back, Lord Furness is coming to see me and he especially wanted to say 'hello' to his friend. He even asked if I had been looking after him properly... I can't possibly tell him we've given the creature away. It's vital you get him back for me.'

But it was not quite that easy. At the hospital I discovered other people had also donated life-sized Snoopys to the children and there were nine possible candidates who could be Tony's friend. I asked the Matron if I could possibly borrow one of the Snoopys as the Cardinal wanted him to be present at a tea party that afternoon. Not surprisingly the Matron looked a little puzzled.

'It will get the Cardinal out of a very difficult situation,' I told her, which probably confused her even more, but she agreed I could take one of the stuffed dogs.

'Though it all sounds very strange to me,' she added.

I wasn't by any means a specialist in Snoopys and had only a vague recollection of the original, but after examining the nine candidates, one seemed more like Tony's friend than the others and I tried to grab him.

But two small children were also hanging on to him and when I tried to pull him away they dug in their heels. 'He's ours,' they screamed, clinging on to one arm and I suddenly found myself, in black suit and a dog collar, wrestling with two angry children to get possession of a giant cartoon canine.

Then one of them started crying and I was quickly surrounded by a hostile group of children, parents and nurses. They were glaring at me and hissing as though I were the wicked villain in a pantomime. I finally won the tug of war and scuttled away with Snoopy over one shoulder, feeling like a criminal. When I got back to the Cardinal's study I was still feeling wretched.

'I've just been booed out of the Children's Hospital and been accused of stealing the children's toys,' I told him. 'After all that, I hope Lord Furness is happy to see him.' But of course he wasn't...

Snoopy had inevitably suffered by being manhandled by countless children and was looking somewhat shabby. Even after I brushed him and sat him in the Cardinal's armchair he did not look in great shape. Tony was horrified when he saw him.

'You haven't been looking after him very well' he told the Cardinal accusingly. 'I had expected him to find a good home here.'

'I introduced him to some of the young choristers, who are a bit boisterous,' the Cardinal replied nervously, telling the small fib I had thought up a few minutes before Tony arrived. But Tony was not so easily appeased. 'I made a big mistake leaving him here,' he said. 'The best thing I can do is take him back home with me.' Fortunately, the neglect of Snoopy did not prevent him making his usually generous donation to the Cathedral funds, but it is the reason why the children at the hospital never saw that particular Snoopy again.

Cardinal Hume was rarely unsettled by the people with whom he came into contact, but there was one person – who stood lower than his chest – of whom he was quite terrified. Mother Theresa of Calcutta, now Blessed Theresa of Calcutta. It was said that no cardinal in the world was safe when it came to dealing with her. She was highly skilled at getting people to part with the things she wanted.

'Even the Pope is terrified when Mother Theresa comes visiting with her latest shopping list,' confided Basil Hume, who was like putty before every meeting with her.

'She always wants things,' he groaned. 'And I always give them to her.'

At one early meeting she asked for a thirty-bedroom house in London to establish a centre for AIDS victims; Hume gave her the money.

She was highly skilled at getting people to part with the things she wanted and he was highly nervous before every visit speculating on the demands she would be making – and the cost to the Church. Of course necessary elements for sanctity!

The last time she had come to visit, he surprised me by personally escorting her to the front door of Archbishop's House where a stretch limousine, sent by Princess Diana, was waiting at the kerb for her. He had a spring in his step and looked quite pleased with himself. As the tiny nun disappeared into the luxurious depths of the huge stretch limo he said to me in a stage whisper, 'To think, the tiniest woman in the world getting into the largest car in the world.' And as it drew away he closed the door and said, 'Thank the Lord. All she wanted this time was a monstrance – and not another mansion,' as he grinned widely.

A monstrance is a cross-shaped container for the Consecrated Host which has an opening through which the Host can be viewed. A few hundred pounds and not a few hundred thousand! Sighs of relief all round.

Hume's 'people' would make their appearance at the oddest of moments. One such was in 1994 when I happened, almost literally, to bump into him in Vatican City. I was on my way to lunch at our Roman friary, being driven rather erratically in a tiny car by my then Director of Studies, Belgian Monsignor André Joos, when we almost ran over two men who had stepped into the road as we left the Vatican.

It was Cardinal Hume accompanied by Cardinal Ratzinger,

who is, of course, now Pope. Had the Monsignor been a second or two later applying the brakes there might never have been a Benedict XVI at all, and no more Basil Hume. As it was, the pair were almost on our bonnet when he screeched to a halt. Both jaywalking cardinals stared in through the windscreen accusingly, clearly believing the near accident to have been our fault. Then I saw Hume visibly start when he recognized me.

I don't think he even knew I was in Rome. Ratzinger merely offered a curt nod. Hume had obviously been shaken by the incident and was also angry and stormed round to my side of the car.

I lowered the window and said, 'Hello, how nice to see you.' No point at all in trying to point out that we were blameless. The Cardinal raised his clenched fist and in his drunken Irish voice shouted, 'Assassins! Filthy assassins! You were trying to kill us both. It's a Protestant plot!'

Our future Pope looked rather bewildered – as did my driver. Better drive on, I told the Monsignor. I'll explain everything over lunch, and we sped on our way, leaving Cardinal Hume shaking his fist after us. I wonder if Ratzinger ever received an explanation.

Although leading the 'opposition' as head of the Church of England, the Queen was always a great admirer and supporter of Cardinal Hume. In fact the whole Royal Family shared her esteem for the Cardinal and always spoke of him in warm and affectionate terms. Diana, Princess of Wales was especially fond of him and often called in to Archbishop's House for a chat or to pray with the Cardinal during the most trying moments of her troubled life. The Cardinal was always able to provide comfort and reassurance for her when she was feeling particularly distressed.

She was also a great champion of The Passage, the centre for the homeless in Victoria which the Cardinal founded in the 1980s. Since arriving in London he had been concerned about the many homeless people he encountered while taking his regular walks around the capital's central streets. Initially he encouraged them to sleep in the Cathedral Piazza at night, away from the traffic, but told me this was not good enough. We needed to do more. One particularly bleak winter's night he went out to the Piazza where dozens of tragic figures huddled under blankets and newspapers trying to keep warm in the freezing temperatures and was so upset by their plight that he invited them all to sleep in the Cathedral Hall – it was discovered later that he had previously been hiding some of the homeless in the Cathedral's crypt at night without telling the Cathedral authorities.

It could only be a temporary solution as the Hall was in almost constant demand as a church and community centre, and couldn't properly double as a night shelter for the homeless. But having embarked on his mission of help, the Cardinal was determined to find an alternative venue which could become a permanent night stop for the human flotsam of London's West End. This was the start of The Passage.

Diana was a supporter right from the beginning and would visit frequently, arriving alone and unheralded and without any fuss, usually between eight and nine in the evening. She would sit and talk with the homeless and discuss their problems with them and, as soon as her sons William and Harry were old enough, she brought them with her. The boys would play games with the occupants – cards or checkers or darts – while Diana did the rounds, talking.

The Cardinal was very saddened when she died and mourned her loss right up to the time of his own death two years later. The night before her funeral in Westminster Abbey, Cardinal Hume celebrated a Requiem Mass for Diana in the Cathedral. Her sisters and Frances Shand Kydd did the readings, and the then Archbishop of Canterbury, George Carey, was present.

I met with Frances on several occasions when she visited London, the last time being a year before she died, when we spent hours together, talking over lunch. She was tormented and torn by the utter tragedy and pain of Diana's death - while at the same time trying always to strive for the positive. Shortly after becoming a Catholic, Frances began regularly accompanying groups of handicapped children and young adults to Lourdes. She was a deeply caring person and I know there was a great deal of depth and love within her broken-ness. Though she would never, in this life, possibly resolve or understand the complexities surrounding her daughter's death. I hope and pray that there is now that peace and understanding between them that was lacking in this life.

The Cathedral was packed for the Mass for Diana and the Cardinal preached the homily, which was a little controversial: it was given as though he was speaking to Diana, with him saying: 'We all loved you, because we knew you were flawed.' It brought out her humanity and everyone loved it.

The Times printed the full text of his sermon the following morning and when Hume attended the funeral he was warmly applauded as he entered the Abbey. I watched the funeral procession from the roof of the Cathedral with our then Cathedral Administrator, George Stack (sometimes known as Obadiah Slope [the Bishop's sinister chaplain in Trollope's *Barchester Chronicles*]). We saw the procession leave the Palace and go along the Mall on its way to the Abbey, not being able to see it along the whole route, but catching glimpses along the way.

The end for Cardinal Hume came quickly and totally unexpectedly and the shock was all that much greater because he had always seemed so fit and active and full of life. In 1999, on Easter Sunday, he hosted a lunch for everyone in Cathedral Clergy House, as he did every year. But on this occasion he didn't linger to chat to everyone afterwards, as was normally the case, as he was dashing off to Hertfordshire to visit one of our oldest bishops, James O'Brien (known as Bishop Jim) who had been diagnosed as having cancer and given only a short time to live by his doctors. Ironically, Bishop Jim lived on until 2007 but the Cardinal, whose cancer was discovered shortly after that visit, was dead within two months.

In typical style, Hume elected personally to inform all his priests and bishops of his illness before there was any public announcement. It was done in the form of a very beautiful letter which was both upbeat and happy. God had granted him two graces, he wrote. Time to prepare; and time to meet him.

At the end of the brief letter he instructed everyone, 'Above all, no fuss'. Sadness was not everyone's reaction to the news. After being diagnosed with cancer, Cardinal Hume said he telephoned Timothy Wright, the Abbot of Ampleforth, to tell him. The Abbot said in response, 'Congratulations! That's brilliant news.

I wish I was coming with you.' Hume said he replied, 'Thank you, Timothy. Everyone else has burst into tears.'

For most, however, the news of Cardinal Hume's impending death was a cause for great sorrow, and two men who were genuinely affected by the announcement were Princes Andrew and Edward. I spoke with them at length during the reception following a wedding at which I was the celebrant. The bride was a close friend of all three of the Queen's sons, but Charles was unable to attend. It was very shortly after we had learned about the Cardinal's illness and most of my conversation with the Princes that day was about him. Both commented on his kindness and how saintly he was, and it was obvious they were not merely being trivial or polite but were speaking with real feeling. They showed a serious understanding and recognition of the Cardinal's qualities, and it was impressive to hear from them how much he would be missed – by millions of Anglicans as well as his own flock.

That the Queen shared her sons' admiration and esteem for Cardinal Hume was never in doubt, and she demonstrated this most effectively by bestowing on him the Order of Merit, an award in her personal gift. The Order is limited to the Sovereign and just twenty-four members which makes it one of the most special of all the honours.

By this time, only a month after he was first diagnosed with cancer, it was so advanced that he had been moved to the Catholic hospital of St John and St Elizabeth in St John's Wood, North London. I had said my last 'goodbye' the day before he left Archbishop's House for hospital and just days before I was to fly out to America for the five-yearly Chapter of my order – the Franciscans of the Atonement, based in upstate New York.

I knew that I would not see him again in this lifetime and it was a very emotional and moving farewell. There was an intimacy between us that had never been expressed properly during our twenty years of friendship – but which showed me that it had always been there.

The Cardinal hated being touched – by anyone, even those who helped him into his Cardinal's vestments. If one of them touched him he would go mad. When I arrived in his study he motioned me to sit in a chair which he had drawn up close to his own. We sat and talked quietly about our years together and some of the momentous events we had experienced in that time and I gradually became overwhelmed by sadness. Even knowing his aversion to being touched I found myself reaching out to cover his hand with mine, and it was a wonderful moment when, instead of jerking his hand away, as I would have expected, he left it there and placed his other hand over my own. It would have been a very simple gesture from anyone else but coming from him it was a remarkable one. The emotion of the moment was just too much for me and I began to cry, which, perversely he found amusing.

'Oh no, not another one,' he laughed. 'We all have to go Michael and you shouldn't worry, just remember me in your prayers, as I will you.' The strength of his faith and his affection rolled over me like warm billowing clouds and for several moments I basked in the spirituality and goodness that seemed to emanate from him.

The very last function he attended was for his beloved Choir School. The Cathedral Choir had won one of the top music prizes in the world at the annual awards ceremony organized by *Gramophone*, the prestigious classical music magazine, at the

Royal Festival Hall. The choir, under its then Master of Music, James O'Donnell, won the award in the choral category and then went on to receive the greatest of all accolades, the Record of the Year award.

They had eliminated 5,000 other entries on their way to the top prize, previously won by Pavarotti. Despite his advanced illness, and being very weak, the Cardinal insisted on hosting the reception for the choir in the Throne Room. All thirty choristers, plus twelve lay adult singers, were there and he spoke to every one of them individually. It was a deeply emotional evening and by the end of the reception everyone, save the Cardinal himself, was in tears.

Hume adored the Choir School and went there virtually every day if he was at home. That was his real life, he always told me, and he loved it. He said he entered into a world of normality when he went there. He would stroll around the playground and all the children would come up to him and talk to him and he would help them with their Latin and other subjects. It was going back to his roots at beloved Ampleforth.

The Choir School was the oasis of his whole life at Westminster and it was an amazing coincidence that it should be the focus of his last official reception in Archbishop's House. It gave him the opportunity to thank and praise James O'Donnell for being such an outstanding Master of Music. James didn't know it at the time but Hume had already proposed him to become a Knight Commander of the Order of St Gregory the Great – a very high Papal knighthood, which he would receive after the Cardinal died. Shortly after that reception he was gone from Archbishop's House.

The Cardinal was destined to return to his home one final time before his death – to prepare for his visit to Buckingham Palace to receive his Order of Merit from the Queen. The Prince of Wales had offered to take his medal to the hospital after doctors advised he was not strong enough to travel to the Palace, but the Cardinal was adamant. If his sovereign was gracious enough to bestow on him this award, then he must go to her personally to receive it. And he did.

But first he was driven from the hospital to Archbishop's House to be dressed for the event. The whole household lined up to greet him. He chose his black cassock with the scarlet buttons and the scarlet sash and was then driven to the Palace for his hour alone with the Queen. Afterwards he went back to the hospital in St John's Wood and remained there until his death on Thursday, June 17th.

I returned to England a week before he died but by this time he was seeing only his Private Secretary, Monsignor Jim Curry, who had been with him for six years, and his sister Madeleine, Lady Hunt and other members of the family.

At 5pm on that Thursday the bells of Westminster Cathedral were tolled and it was packed within minutes. The Duchess of Kent, sobbing inconsolably as she prayed, was one of the first to arrive. She was finally comforted by a young man, a Cathedral volunteer. It was a scene repeated throughout the Cathedral as grief-stricken parishioners clutched at strangers to ease their distress.

The Cardinal was brought back to Archbishop's House in a hearse and lay quietly in his private chapel in an open coffin, dressed in his Benedictine habit and with his ring and pallium, the white, sheep's wool band, peculiar to an archbishop and a sign of his association with the Pope, that is worn around the neck. Only family and close friends saw him there and he looked utterly at peace.

In a remarkable tribute *The Times* newspaper said, 'Few churchmen in this century, inside or outside the Catholic Church have died more deeply loved than Cardinal Basil Hume. He had become the nation's spiritual leader; not intentionally, but by virtue of his personal holiness, his Benedictine spirituality, and by way of holding office for over 23 years'.

From the Sunday his closed coffin rested in the library in Clergy House close to the Choir School and on Monday it was moved to the Cathedral Hall where the public were invited to pay their last respects. The whole of Ambrosden Avenue bordering the south side of the Cathedral was cordoned off by police as tens of thousands of people queued to file past the Cardinal's coffin. Different groups, including the Chelsea Pensioners and the Papal Knights took turns to mount a guard of honour around the coffin. On top was his scarlet Cardinal's biretta and nearby on a cushion was his Order of Merit, a red cross surmounted by a golden crown.

The procession heading his last entry into the Cathedral comprised representatives of virtually every Church and faith on earth. The Cardinals of Milan, Paris, Holland and Ireland were there and dozens of bishops from around the world. The then Archbishop of Canterbury, George Carey and former Archbishop Robert Runcie were robed, with the Russian and Greek Orthodox Archbishops, Anthony Bloom and Gregorios. There were Christians, Jews, Muslims, Buddhists, Methodists,

Baptists, Salvationists and just about every other faith you could think of. The Prime Ministers of Britain and Ireland attended and the Queen sent the Duchess of Kent to represent her. The Chief Rabbi was in attendance watching proceedings from a television in Archbishop's House. Also there was former punk receptionist Brian, paying his last respects.

Representing the Pope was the celebrant, Australian Cardinal Edward Cassidy, President of the Pontifical Council for Christian Unity in the Vatican, who read out a beautiful personal letter from Pope John Paul II. The Cathedral was filled to overflowing and the full, two-hour service was broadcast live on BBC television. Hundreds of people stood in the Piazza in front of the Cathedral listening to the Mass. Fittingly it was one of the Cardinal's closest friends, John Crowley, Bishop of Middlesbrough who gave the sermon. He had served the Cardinal for many years at Archbishop's House as his Private Secretary before being made a bishop in London in 1985. Hume had then transferred him to Middlesbrough (which had Ampleforth Abbey in its Diocese), for it is thought he had intended to retire to his old abbey and wanted his friend John Crowley to be close by. He probably would have helped him in the Diocese.

In his sermon John Crowley spoke of the Cardinal's goodness and charismatic spirituality though suddenly cut himself short. He told me later he knew the Cardinal would have been very annoyed with him because he was making him seem to be a saint. He told the congregation, 'I can feel the Cardinal pulling at my cassock telling me to stop.' And so he did. He ended the sermon right there.

He was so right about Hume, and I was reminded of the Cardinal's expression: 'Enjoy, but don't inhale.' It very much summarized Hume's attitude: 'Don't let it go to your head.'

He never let it go to his.

$\mathscr{S}$IX

THE SCARLET DUO – JOKER AND THE QUEEN –
BLIND MAN'S BLUFF – PIKES, STICKS AND
GROWLING DOGS – QUEEN'S HAT TAKES A KNOCK –
A STEP TOO FAR – WHEN THE PRESIDENT
PATTED THE QUEEN'S RUMP

The first time I was presented to the Queen, the then Cathedral Administrator warned her not to talk to me, because I was too dangerous. It happened in 1995 during a reception in the Throne Room in Archbishop's House following a service to commemorate the Cathedral's centenary.

The Queen became the first British monarch officially to attend a Catholic service, in this case Latin Vespers – or evening prayer – since the 16th century. She was dressed from head to toe in scarlet, as was the Cardinal who was wearing his full scarlet regalia, including his scarlet skullcap.

Each must have received a shock when the Cardinal went to greet her at the main entrance to the Cathedral, for their outfits mirrored each other like a double act out of a Gilbert and Sullivan operetta – even the difference in their height was slightly comical. There were audible gasps from the congregation as they caught sight of the matched pair. Fortunately, the Queen's distinctive black handbag was not something with which the Cardinal could compete.

After the forty-five minute service, the Queen and the Duchess of Kent, who had been present too, joined Church leaders in the Throne Room in Archbishop's House for a reception. We all stood in little groups of ten or more and I was in a circle with the then Administrator, Monsignor George Stack, who had done much of the work leading up to the Queen's visit.

Normally at that time on a Thursday evening the Throne Room would have been full of Anglican clergy who were 'crossing over' following the decision of the Anglican Church to ordain women priests. We were giving them gentle refreshers in theology – bits and pieces they would need before being ordained as Catholic priests, like Canon Law (the guide book of the Catholic Church), and other subjects. Not all were 'High Church' and up to speed on things; indeed, some were very 'Low Church' but we had assembled a group of distinguished scholars and priests to help them through the transition.

The previous Thursday I had told them that their boss, the Supreme Governor of the Church of England, the Queen, needed the Throne Room the following week and we would have to evict them temporarily. So on the night the Queen was attending the reception, her former vicars were tucked away in a local convent, St Vincent's, in nearby Carlisle Place, above The Passage, our centre for the homeless, receiving instruction which would help them transfer from the Church of England.

The Queen was fully aware of what was going on, but the general consensus had been that it was better, or at least more correct, not to mention the subject to her.

That was the position as Cardinal Hume approached our group with the Queen and began the presentations. When it came to my turn I shook her hand and bowed my head and said, 'Good evening Your Majesty,' as I had been directed.

Then George Stack, ever the joker, stepped forward, and in a loud voice told her, 'Ma'am have nothing to do with him. He's dangerous!'

I felt my face burn – probably turning the colour of the Queen's and the Cardinal's outfits – and I couldn't think of a word to say. It was quite mortifying. This was very much a private joke, for the Queen didn't have the slightest idea what he was talking about, but she gave me a long, hard look as she was led away to meet the Duke of Norfolk and some of the other guests. But she kept glancing back at me, and when the Cardinal moved on towards the next circle of people, she didn't follow him but walked back to me.

'Father, why did he say that you are dangerous?' she asked.

It was, of course, the million dollar question, which we had decided none of us would talk about. I could see George Stack and the Cardinal and the Queen's Lady-in-waiting hovering nearby, but none of them wanted to rush in and grab her and tell her to move on. So it was up to me to reply.

'I think, Your Majesty, it is because I have been involved in the journeys of quite a few of your Church of England clergy towards the Catholic Church and I don't think we should be talking about this on such a lovely occasion. Though a number of lay people, like Her Royal Highness,' and here I gestured towards the Duchess of Kent, 'have already "crossed over" and many more lay people and clergy are considering the move.'

'Yes,' said the Queen, 'and I know you are being most helpful in assisting them on their journey.'

'Some people feel that this is what they must do,' I said. 'We must all of us remember to keep a balance and remain friendly.'

'Absolutely,' she replied. 'They are only obeying their consciences.'

I said: 'Actually, Your Majesty, tonight they send their love and respect to you. Normally they would be in this room for their classes in becoming Catholic priests. They can't be here tonight, of course, because you are here. We had to evict them temporarily in your honour. It might have been rather indelicate to have had them here tonight. They are over in the nearby convent instead.'

'That's very interesting,' she said, 'but please remember me to them all, Father, and say I am very grateful they have given up this nice room for me. It's a very sensitive matter.'

'Yes, very delicate,' I said. 'But I will pass on your message to them all.'

'Well, they are only doing what they feel they must,' she said, 'and I am so glad that you have explained this to me.'

Meanwhile over her shoulder, I could see the Cardinal and the others waiting. She was delaying everything to talk with me, but showed no signs of wanting to move on. Everyone was staring at us during our chat, the one conversation no-one had planned to have with her. If it hadn't been for the Cardinal making funny faces at me, we might have gone on talking for the whole evening. 'I think, Your Majesty, that they may want you to meet other people...' She gave a glance over her shoulder at the waiting group and turned back to me and smiled. 'You're not a dangerous man at all Father. What you are doing is very helpful to many troubled people, my people, and I thank you for it.'

And she carried on chatting for a few moments longer – I think just to let people know who was boss – then rejoined her escorts.

Later Cardinal Hume wanted to know exactly what had been said and when I told him, he smiled and said: 'Michael, that's just the kind of sensitive response I would expect from her. She has incredible understanding and compassion for people, which is why she's such a great monarch.'

Astonishingly, that was not the only time I was instrumental in throwing the Queen's schedule into chaos, for on yet another memorable occasion she decided to engage me in a lengthy chat during a reception.

This time it was at St James's Palace given in honour of the Royal Institute for the Blind. I had been invited as a 'minder' for Father Norman Brown, a blind priest then resident at the Cathedral; he didn't have a guide dog and asked if I would be his guide. He can just about make out shapes but needs to walk with a white stick.

Anyone who has been to a reception at St James's Palace will know that the formal rooms comprise a number of inter-connected large rooms, and that for a big reception all the doors are thrown back to make one large space.

There were well over three hundred people there so I advised Norman that our chances of actually meeting the Queen were pretty slim. But I promised I would keep up a running commentary of what was going on so he would have a good souvenir of the event in his mind. I assumed she would spend most of her time talking to the big donors who were present, most of whom were sighted. We talked to Rolf Harris and also said hello to Cilla Black and Ronnie Corbett, all of whom are supporters of the Institute.

All the blind people wanted to know what the Queen was wearing and we could judge her approach by the volume of the whispers as information was passed forward from person to person. All we could hear, getting stronger, were the words 'blue; blue; blue!'

'I think we can safely assume she is wearing blue,' I told Norman.

Suddenly the Queen was in our room with His Grace The Duke of Westminster doing the presentations. What seemed very funny to me was that the Queen was flanked by four Yeomen of the Guard, in full uniform and carrying pikes, who were marching along with her, in a room full of blind people who could not see the pomp and spectacle of it all.

Even funnier because the pikes and blind people's sticks occasionally connected and set the blind dogs amongst them growling!

I suppose Father Norman, in his black cassock, snow white hair and kindly face, and me in my brown friar's habit must have stood out slightly from the other booted and suited figures for I could see that the Queen had spotted us as soon as she entered the room.

She was supposed to be listening to someone else, but kept glancing in our direction and suddenly she broke away from The Duke of Westminster and her Yeomen and strode straight towards us.

I could see her but Norman couldn't, and I had no chance to

warn him for it seemed in a flash that she was standing before us. The Yeomen, unsure whether to regroup around her, eventually formed a guard six feet away, blocking off the Duke's view.

I just said, 'Your Majesty,' and took her outstretched hand and bowed my head. I knew one shouldn't do that unless one had been properly presented, but she couldn't introduce herself because she was the Queen.

'I'm Father Michael Seed from Westminster Cathedral,' I said.

Norman, who didn't hear me, did not know what was going on.

'Father Brown, this is the Queen,' I yelled.

'The Queen?' he shouted back.

'Yes, the Queen,' I hissed, 'and this is her hand.'

'Oh, Your Majesty,' he simpered, grasping her hand in both of his, stepping forward and giving his most profound bow. He was slightly taller than the Queen and so close to her that his forehead struck the front of the sovereign's hat and knocked it down over her brow. Members of the Royal Household visibly blanched. The Yeomen's pikes quivered.

The Queen just laughed and pushed her hat back up. Her Lady-in-waiting, still hanging back, looked slightly nonplussed.

'And where are you from, Father Brown?' the Queen enquired.

'I am from Westminster Cathedral,' he said proudly.

'Oh, you're with dear Cardinal Hume,' she said. 'He is such a wonderful man. Please, do give him my deepest regards.'

She was clearly in one of those moods when she had found someone she wanted to talk to, and had decided to let the devil take her schedule. She stayed and chatted with us for several minutes more, asking us about our work at the Cathedral and saying lovely things about the Cardinal and what he was achieving. Everything else went on hold until she decided it was time to move on.

It was a brief but totally unexpected encounter and she left behind her two dedicated and adoring royalists, as she was escorted off by her Yeomen, in their flanking positions, leaving white sticks in disarray and dogs growling.

Again, a remarkable lady.

One other connection I had with the Royal Family was through a man called Victor Fletcher, who was a senior member of the 'backstairs team' at Buckingham Palace, whom I had first met in 1985 when I was still a deacon at the Cathedral. He had his own small flat in the Palace up in the top south-west corner, and would often invite me there for large gins and tonic, his favoured tipple.

One could reach the lift to his flat by going through the Queen's Gallery entrance and through the vast lower staff area which had its own café, restaurant, and full sports facilities, including pool tables and table tennis. Once a year at Christmas, Victor would invite a dozen priests for dinner at the Rubens Hotel near the Palace, and we would reciprocate by inviting back those who wished it, to have drinks with us at Cathedral Clergy House.

Victor had been received into the Catholic Church shortly before we first met and told me the Queen had been very understanding and said she would remember him in her prayers. She gave him a prayer book to commemorate his reception.

Victor had originally worked for the Queen's father, King George VI, and had known Elizabeth since she was a little girl. He had known hundreds of servants pass through the Palace and told me they never openly advertised for new staff. The adverts were placed in provincial newspapers in places like Liverpool and were completely anonymous so people wouldn't know they were applying for a job at Buckingham Palace.

Victor particularly liked to go with the Family to Balmoral and loved to spend whole days going for long walks alone across the moors, with a flask and sandwiches. He was a very contemplative and reflective person and fiercely loyal to the Queen, whom he adored. He was also a great admirer of the Prince of Wales whom he believed would one day make a fine monarch.

But not every royal with whom he came into contact was so popular. Victor told me that on one occasion when a number of people had been invited to stay at Windsor Castle, a particular couple caused consternation. The Queen had, as always, assigned bedrooms to her guests for the weekend. One suite which was never assigned to guests, was affectionately known as The Queen Mother's Bedroom; even though the Queen Mother lived a few minutes' drive away at Windsor Royal Lodge, the Queen always kept that suite of rooms free for her, should she ever want to stay.

On this occasion, one royal couple considered the room that they had been allocated did not correctly reflect their status. So the wife had gone searching the rooms until she found one which she believed to be more suitable. Unbeknownst to her, she had chosen the Queen Mother's suite and before she could be alerted to her double *faux pas*, had moved all her and her husband's luggage from what she considered her allocated 'inferior' rooms.

Victor was speechless. 'When I asked her to move the luggage back to the room she had been given, she refused point blank and told me she was staying put,' he said.

125

Not knowing what else to do, he went straight to the Queen, who was preparing for dinner and was wearing just a simple bathrobe. Learning of the room swap, Queen Elizabeth stormed off down the corridors just as she was, and marched straight into The Queen Mother's Bedroom, and, in front of the presumptuous guests, ordered their luggage to be thrown out, whether it was packed or unpacked.

'I had never seen her so angry,' said Victor.

Then, with a face like thunder, he said, she ordered the suitably chastised royal couple back to their assigned quarters. Normally people were very respectful towards the Queen, said Victor, but there were exceptions. Not people being deliberately rude, but just being themselves. One such was the loveable President Ronald Reagan. It happened on the Royal Yacht Britannia and the President and his wife had been guests of honour for dinner.

After dinner the Queen decided that she, herself, would serve the coffee to people, which was most unusual.

'In that situation you would imagine that any guest would take anything she offered,' said Victor. 'But when she asked President Reagan if he would like a coffee, she was stunned when he replied: "No thanks. Do you have a decaff?"

'That would have been affront enough, but as someone was dispatched to find a decaffeinated coffee, Reagan reached out a hand and gently patted the Queen on the rump, and said: "Thanks for taking care of that."

'Everyone held their breath waiting for the explosion,' said Victor, 'but it never came. The Queen just smiled and said: "That's perfectly alright Mister President.".'

I understand the whole Royal Family mourned the death of

Victor. He had, several times over the years, shown me a large scrapbook filled with handwritten thank-you letters from virtually every member of the Royal Family going back some fifty years. He died of cancer in the Brompton Hospital twenty years ago and I went to see him there to say my goodbyes. Princess Diana had been just before I arrived. Victor had seen how lost she seemed and had taken her under his wing when she first moved in to Buckingham Palace, and taught her the royal ropes when she was feeling out of her depth. They all had a lot to thank him for.

$\mathscr{S}$EVEN

CARDINAL IN A TIZZY – ARCHBISHOP 'BEAN' OF
CANTERBURY – BLACKADDER FOR HIS EMINENCE –
PANIC IN THE VESTRY – LUCKY DIP

The Archbishop of Canterbury, Dr Rowan Williams, is a
serious academic and a respected theologian, as well as being
an accomplished and published poet. I was not, therefore,
anticipating a particularly entertaining journey when we
travelled together to St Albans and back by car – and had
resigned myself to the expected tedium. My fear was all the more
so as we were to be accompanied by the President of the
Vatican's Pontifical Council for Christian Unity, Cardinal Walter
Kasper, former Bishop of Stuttgart, Germany.

It was not until that day in May 2003 that I was to spend any
length of time in the company of the 104th Archbishop of
Canterbury since his appointment five months earlier. He is the
first ever Welshman to get the job, and, like most English people,
I had heard that his countrymen are not always noted for their
light-hearted approach to life. But instead of my anticipated

nightmare, our drive to St Albans turned out to be one of the funniest journeys of my life.

It transpired that Rowan Williams has an outrageous sense of humour and he had me shaking and spluttering with laughter all the way with his schoolboy humour, but left Cardinal Kasper convinced that the Archbishop was possibly deranged.

With others, I had helped to organize a conference for Christian Unity, on 17 May 2003, at St Alban's Abbey, a place dedicated to the first martyr in England when the country was under the Roman occupation. The then 53-year-old Archbishop and the Cardinal, himself a distinguished theologian (who had represented the Pope at Williams' Enthronement), were to be two of the main guest speakers.

I had suggested to Dr Williams (who had kindly agreed to transport the German Cardinal) that it might be nice, and friendlier, if he picked us up from Archbishop's House, where Cardinal Kasper was staying with Cardinal Cormac, and then drive us to St Albans. We had decided to leave at 7.30am so as to arrive early and I was waiting outside Archbishop's House when a family people-carrier car arrived with Williams and his ecumenical secretary, Canon Jonathan Gough, seated in the back.

Cardinal Cormac hadn't known what to do about the Archbishop's fleeting visit. Given that Cardinal Kasper was only being collected, there was really no reason for Cardinal Cormac to come to the door of Archbishop's House at all to say hello. Nonetheless, he was in a quandary about whether he should greet the Archbishop formally inside or, as the Archbishop was on this occasion offering a 'taxi service', wait out on the street, with Kasper and me, and simply say 'hello'. The two cardinals had tossed the question around for at least fifteen minutes and it was becoming ridiculous.

'It doesn't really matter,' I told him. 'There is no protocol for this.'

But being the courteous man he is, Cormac concluded that he should be there to greet the Archbishop of Canterbury – so that's what happened...

As the car stopped outside, I told Dr Williams that the Cardinal wanted to see him and he jumped out, wearing a plain cassock with his pectoral cross, and followed me up the steps of Archbishop's House and inside, to where the two cardinals were waiting in the reception area. But I was so wound up with dear Cardinal Cormac's indecision about where (if at all) to greet the new Archbishop, I botched the introduction.

'Your Eminences,' I said, 'may I present the Archbishop of Canterbury, Doctor Rowan Atkinson.' Rowan Williams gave me a hard stare and I suddenly realized I had introduced him as the popular comedy actor – of *Mr Bean* fame.

My gaffe definitely didn't register with Cardinal Kasper and I don't think it even registered with Cormac, because he was so befuddled anyway. But as soon as we were settled in the car – the Cardinal and the Archbishop on the seats behind the driver, and Jonathan and I on the seats behind them – I apologized:

'I'm sorry, your Grace, for presenting you as Rowan Atkinson.'

'Not at all,' came the reply. 'I took it as a compliment. I adore *Mr Bean* and Rowan Atkinson and I've seen every episode of *Blackadder*.' And that's how the amusement – and bemusement – started.

It emerged that Dr Williams really <u>did</u> know every episode of the comedy series and began to recount the funniest scenes from each, even mimicking some of the voices. The German Cardinal was mystified by the imaginary character we were discussing and seemed almost mesmerized by the bearded, windmill-armed, giggling man next to him. The Archbishop, it appeared, had a marked Rabelaisian preference in his humour, and extolled the erotic episodes of *Blackadder* as being the funniest.

'Shall we tell His Eminence about the episode where Blackadder becomes Archbishop of Canterbury?' I suggested. 'Oh splendid!' came Dr Williams's reply.

He and I then launched into a detailed description of the story, set in the Tudor period, when the King lay dying surrounded by the Princes and one was to be made King, another to be Prince of Wales and others to be Royal Dukes or whatever. Blackadder is the only one left without a title, not to mention land and money, and pleads, 'Don't die without telling me what I'm going to get!' The King replies, 'Oh, I'd forgotten about you. You will be Archbishop of Canterbury.' 'I don't believe in God,' replies Blackadder. 'That has nothing to do with it. You get lots of land,' says the King, and promptly dies.

In the said episode, you then see Blackadder begin a tour of the monasteries, pillaging...

By this time, Cardinal Kaspar was looking thoroughly befuddled, and the more we tried to explain, the more bewildered he became, and clearly did not understand why the two of us were cackling with laughter.

'Do you think we should mention Blackadder's special clothing to His Eminence?' I asked the Archbishop.

'I don't think it would be really appropriate,' he told me, but was by this time so engrossed in the re-enactment of his favourite television programme, he spontaneously launched into a series of detailed hand gestures of Blackadder's codpiece. Despite our best efforts – not surprising given our laughter – we somehow failed to enlighten the Papal Emissary. By this time, I am certain that he was convinced Rowan Williams was crazy and that he was trapped in a car with a pair of dangerous British lunatics. Jonathan Gough had sensibly remained silent.

The Cardinal looked most apprehensive and had shrunk away from the Archbishop, towards the door. When we reached St Albans, Williams and I both with aching sides from laughing, Kasper shot out of the car with Jonathan, and scuttled off into the Abbey at top speed – obviously much relieved to have escaped his deranged travelling companions.

But a far more serious and practical personal problem presented him after the conference as we prepared for Choral Evensong. Cardinal Kasper had borrowed a case from Cardinal Cormac's then Private Secretary, Monsignor Mark O'Toole, to carry his regalia for the ceremony. His scarlet cassock, cape and zucchetto (the little skullcap worn by bishops and others in the Catholic Church) and other bits and pieces were inside the executive-like case – and they looked like staying there. Someone, somehow, had managed to fiddle with the combination locks of the two flaps which wrapped around the case and we couldn't open it.

Everyone else in the vestry was getting prepared for the service, including the Archbishop of Canterbury and the Bishop of St Albans, Christopher Herbert – but not the Cardinal, one of the principle guests, who was furious and refusing to 'go on' unless he was 'properly dressed'.

I telephoned London and tried to contact Cardinal Cormac's Secretary, but he was away, and no-one else knew the combination of his case.

The Catholic Bishop of Hertfordshire, Jim O'Brien, who was wearing 'standard' purple, approached Kasper and said, 'You can have my things Your Eminence.'

'No. I would look ridiculous,' snapped the irate Cardinal. And so he would, I could see that: Jim was six feet two inches and Kasper was barely five foot. With hems and sleeves trailing he could have looked like Dopey of the Seven Dwarfs. But for Kasper I think it was the colour which worried him most. 'I wear scarlet,' he shouted at everyone, 'scarlet, not purple!' The discrepancy in their sizes appeared not to have occurred to him.

While he was complaining, the Archbishop of Canterbury and the Bishop of St Albans, both in their full regalia, had each seized a strap of the stubbornly locked case and were leaning at angles away from one another having a tug-of-war. It was like a scene from an Ealing comedy, but at the time no-one dared laugh. Suddenly one of the locks popped open and Williams and Herbert cheered. Cardinal Kasper worked his hand under the edge and managed to pull out his scarlet sash. But that was all.

Meanwhile nearly three thousand people in the congregation had already been kept waiting for fifteen minutes.

In the interim, the verger at St Alban's brought over a white alb (a garment like a cassock) to show Kasper but he refused it. Then the verger brought a black cassock and that too was refused. At which point Williams succeeded in forcing his arm into the case and pulled out a cape. Minutes later, taking his turn, Kasper worked his scarlet skullcap loose. In this lucky-dip style fashion, it came to my turn and I was able to tug free the corner of Kasper's cassock. However, the cassock was rolled up and too fat to pull free in one go but, eventually, with the Archbishop hugging the case and me gently pulling on the aforementioned garment, we managed slowly to unroll it and reveal it inch by inch. We were almost half an hour late starting the service, but at least the Cardinal was in scarlet, and in the right-sized clothes (even if they were somewhat creased). Predictably our journey back to London was one of the quietest of my experience...

EIGHT

THE WHISKY-DRINKING PRIEST – MILLION POUND
CONVERSION – MILITARY MANOEUVRES IN THE
GARDEN – BRING BACK THE BLESSED MARGARET –
TEA WITH SINN FÉIN – A BUDGET TEA PARTY

Being a friend of the late Alan Clark was unpredictable, stimulating and often intriguing –but not always comfortable. He frequently thought in stereotypes and unthinkingly would replace the real person with his mental perception.

Unfortunately for me, he was a great admirer of the works of the novelist Graham Greene, who had always favoured Irish whisky-drinking priests in his works. Alan loved this image and tried to make me fit it. When we first knew one another, he would invite me to meet him in the Pugin Room at the Palace of Westminster at 11am and order very large whiskies, which I did not want at that time in the morning. In Parliamentary bars, they serve double measures as a matter of course, which meant he was ordering quadruple whiskies each time. I was to be his own, Irish whisky-drinking priest, and despite my constant refusals and opposition, he persevered with this notion until he died.

He was a man full of surprises. The first time I went to Saltwood, the thousand-year-old Norman castle his father had bought back in 1955, and from which the knights had set out to murder St Thomas Beckett, it was once again being overrun by military types. We were seated in the main, ancient medieval hall and he sat about twenty feet away from me. It wasn't exactly my idea of an intimate conversation, despite his wanting to discuss something close to his heart.

'I understand I have to give a lot of money to the Catholic Church in order to become a Catholic,' he said.

'Who told you that?' I asked. 'Whoever it was, they were teasing. You don't have to pay a penny!'

'Well I thought I had to, and I was thinking of doing it,' Alan continued, 'though I'm not really worthy of your interest. I'm a very bad person.'

'Good,' I told him. 'The Catholic Church is full of sinners and saints. You have to remember that both Hitler and Mother Theresa were baptized as Catholics.'

I must have said the right thing for he brightened up considerably: I hadn't reckoned on his interest in Adolf Hitler to be quite so strong. It was only later that I noticed there was Nazi memorabilia scattered all over the castle – SS and Gestapo daggers and symbols and armbands in the most unlikely of places. He even told me he had named his dog after Hitler's dog.

He obviously took my remark as a compliment and muttered, 'Wonderful.'

I then tried to explain to him some of the different aspects of theology.

However, while I was talking I spotted, through the window,

men in combat gear and with blacked-out faces, dropping past on ropes. There was also the noise of guns firing and men shouting. Alan sat there intently listening to my exposition of faith, totally ignoring the makings of a *coup d'état* and offered no explanation of what was going on.

Then one of the camouflaged men pointed a machine gun through the window at me and I remarked to Alan, 'The SAS appears to be involved in an armed conflict in your garden.'

'Oh don't worry about them,' he replied nonchalantly. 'They are always here. They use the estate for manoeuvres.'

In hindsight – and out of the sights of the weapons – it was really quite funny and I guess it could only be Alan Clark who would encourage the military to use his home for training purposes...

Alan could be utterly reckless at times. I learned this at first hand, when he was behind the wheel of a car. We had talked late one night at Saltwood and I had missed my last train back to London. Despite the time and distance (Saltwood is near the Kent coast at Deal), he said he would be delighted to drive me home. It would give him the chance to show off one of his collection of vintage cars, which he loved.

His interests in cars – and it would seem strong language – stemmed from his 185 days' National Service in the Household Cavalry, when he acquired a third share in his first Jaguar car.

That night, he strapped on his goggles and we climbed into this open-topped monster, which, he told me proudly, had been built in the 1920s. It was cold and I was soon freezing – as well as terrified. Alan drove very fast and overtook everything on the road. I clung to my seat and a hand strap and remained completely petrified throughout the entire journey, from time to time muttering an act of contrition as yet another near-miss was clocked up. When we reached Victoria, I vowed never to be a passenger with him again.

Under Margaret Thatcher, Alan had been a Minister at the Departments of Trade, Employment and latterly Defence. He idolized her – and not just because he considered her the most sexually attractive woman in politics: 'Eyes, wrists... ankles!' he would exclaim. He was devastated when she was dumped by an ungrateful Tory party and always harboured the hope that she would one day return to power. He even tried to organize a return coup to have her reinstated. I think it was probably a surprise to him (and others) when John Major, who had succeeded Thatcher, reappointed him as a minister, rewarding him with a Privy Counsellorship.

But Alan's particular plot to restore Thatcher lay behind his throwing a large dinner party at Saltwood in 1995, before he returned to the Commons. He had arranged for a chauffeur-driven car to pick up another guest and me from London. My travelling companion was to be the television presenter Selina Scott, a very glamorous lady, who certainly added glitter to the evening.

Jeffrey and Mary Archer were there, as were Michael and Sandra Howard (accompanied by Michael's personal security guards – he was at the time Home Secretary). Fortunately, it was before our 'Something of the Night' falling out, and so we were still on friendly terms. The Nicholsons, tenants of Sissinghurst Castle (now in the care of the National Trust: Sissinghurst's famous gardens were created by Vita Sackville-West, the wife of Harold Nicholson), made up our table.

Alan and his wife, Jane, were brilliant hosts as always and we had already consumed a great deal of champagne when Alan insisted on showing us around his castle, including a stroll on the ruined battlements, which were very high. I refused to go on the battlements, as did Howard's detectives, but the others all managed it, shuffling along in a conga line clutching their champagne glasses. Brave? Yes. But definitely foolhardy.

On reflection, it was obvious that Alan had invited men who shared his feelings for Margaret Thatcher. They were all macho types with beautiful ladies and all adored their former leader. The Conservative Party was by then mired and being pilloried by the media with almost daily reports of sleaze and corruption, and there was a good deal of plotting going on in and around Parliament. Alan, of course, was being outrageous with his plan to bring Maggie back. There is no doubt that at that time she would have been quite capable still of doing the job – but she was already in the House of Lords as Baroness Thatcher. To have had her as Prime Minister while still in the Lords would have been possible, but very odd indeed in 20th century politics. Yet Alan had creative thinking and believed his eccentric plot had merit and that a restoration was quite possible. With Alan, anything seemed possible.

After dinner, when the ladies had withdrawn and the men retreated to the snug for brandies and cigars, Alan mentioned his idea. Although the others knew Alan was capable of suggesting anything, I think they were somewhat taken aback by his mythological suggestion that the legendary Margaret could be reinstated. Michael Howard already had a top job in Government and for this reason alone would never have joined a move against John Major. Jeffrey may have seen a glimmer of enlightenment and a plot would have temporarily appealed to his wicked sense of humour, but I'm sure he would have regained his senses very quickly. Not surprisingly, we were all very late getting away that Saturday night and I was dropped off at Westminster Cathedral a little before 3am after we had deposited the charming Selina Scott outside her home.

Being a Conservative in early 1997 was, I imagine, like being in Hitler's bunker in 1944. They were staring defeat in the face and the only ones who couldn't see it were the ones in charge. Alan's plot died with the decimated Conservative Party in the 1997 General Election. Conversely, of course, Alan adored Tony Blair and thought him a splendid leader, and admired Alastair Campbell whom he had known as a reporter. His candour in admitting these feelings in public could be breathtaking. But I loved his frankness.

Another politician he adored was my good friend Ann Widdecombe, who was nervous of my association with Alan, and warned me to be constantly on my guard with him, as 'he would lead me into mischief'. It was excellent advice.

He truly believed the original IRA leaders at the time of the 1916 Easter Dublin uprising to have been heroes. He said he appreciated their cause for wanting the reunification of Ireland, the fight for 'real liberation'. And in this light he considered the modern IRA not to be the equal of their predecessors – although in October 1984, Alan had what he took to be a providential escape from death when he and Jane, his wife, decided on a whim to leave the Conservative Party Conference a day early. That night, the IRA detonated a 100lb bomb in the

Grand Hotel, sadly killing a number of people and seriously injuring many others.

He never shied from controversy in relation to the IRA and spoke in defence of Bobby Sands, the twenty-seven-year-old IRA hunger striker who had been elected MP for Fermanagh and South Tyrone, who starved himself to death in sixty-six days in the Maze prison in Northern Ireland. Alan could see that it was his prerogative not to take his seat in Westminster as he would be required to swear an oath of allegiance to the Crown, which Alan saw as distinctive from his election to represent the people of his Constituency.

Alan always remained envious of my having been invited to take tea with the Sinn Féin leadership at their headquarters in the Falls Road in Belfast and he pestered me for almost two years to take him and introduce him to the current leaders of Sinn Féin, Gerry Adams and Martin McGuinness. I had, in fact, been entertained by another Sinn Féin member (as Adams and McGuinness were away at the time in Washington visiting President Clinton at the White House).

My invitation to have tea was, I believe, very last minute, and I may have been 'selected' that very day (when they discovered I was to be at St Louise's Comprehensive College to speak on the subject of peace) to have tea in order to become their messenger...

The invitation to speak at the College had been proposed by a top barrister in Ireland, Denis Moloney, who was a governor and, incidentally, a good friend of mine. St Louise's College on the Falls Road in Belfast is the largest single sex school in Europe and was run by the Daughters of Charity of St Vincent de Paul, once known as God's Geese because of their wing-like head coverings.

The girls wore brown uniforms and, at that time, because many of the pupils had fathers linked with the Republican cause, were nicknamed the 'brown bombers'. They sat very quietly throughout, as I talked about my growing up and being a Salvationist and a strict Baptist who considered Ian Paisley to be a dangerous liberal. They laughed, of course, because they didn't have Catholic priests in Belfast with my peculiar religious background.

St Louise's had totally lacked discipline until the arrival of Sister Genevieve who was placed in charge and changed everything. Any girls misbehaving in or outside of school would be cracked down on. They would have to parade outside wearing a sandwich board saying 'I have shamed the school', or face expulsion. It was a remarkable transformation, for which Sister Genevieve was subsequently honoured by the Queen, and the school has now become one of the leading places of education in Ireland, with many students securing places at Oxford and Cambridge universities.

So it was with my invitation to the headquarters of Sinn Féin for tea at 4pm, that I arrived at a house surrounded by barbed wire, with armour-plating and cameras everywhere. The garden was overgrown and filled with discarded equipment and the place looked like a prison. I sat down to a rather formal tea with Sean McKnight and two other city councillors. After some small talk, Mr McKnight read a message to me which said that they understood there were to be more bombings on the mainland, which was really quite alarming. It was 1995 and peace had been tentatively held for about two years and nobody was anticipating a resumption in violence. I was told that this message was to be relayed to the Government in London. I was, not surprisingly, rather shaken.

I went from my afternoon tea to the headquarters of the then RUC to see Sir Ronnie Flanagan, who was at that time the Deputy Commissioner of the Police Service. This extremely humane and entertaining man later became Chief Constable of the Police Service of Northern Ireland, and was until 2008 Chief Inspector of Constabulary in England and Wales. We had a whisky in his office but I didn't mention the message to him because I was rather too alarmed to know what to do. Then I called on another friend, Sir John Wheeler, then Minister of State for Law and Order in Northern Ireland, at Stormont. I didn't mention the message to him either. One reason was that two stenographers were there writing down every single word we said. The civil servants were so paranoid, that no conversations were allowed in Stormont without them being recorded, most especially as I was a Catholic Priest – and you didn't see many of those in Stormont.

My concern was to ensure that the first person who heard my dreadful story and the warning I had been asked to relay, would be someone whose reactions would not be influenced by Northern Irish officialdom.

I took a late plane back to London and immediately called Ann Widdecombe, still a Minister at the Home Office, arranging to see her the next day, the 19th of November. Ann listened to what I had to say and informed the Home Secretary straight away. Various Government people became involved, including

Sir Patrick Mayhew, then Secretary of State for Northern Ireland, as well as the secret services. Having imparted my message, I tried to forget about it, praying that nothing would transpire as a result.

Late in November, Sean McKnight telephoned and asked if I had passed on the message and I told him it had been given to Ann Widdecombe. That seemed to satisfy him. As history relates, on 9 February 1996, the IRA ended a seventeen-month ceasefire with the first of three bomb attacks, two in London and a third devastating blast in Manchester. It was this attack, I believe, which was the subject of my IRA message. It had been my one and only contact with the IRA and I was more than content to let it remain so. But not so Alan Clark...

He wanted to go to Belfast and visit these people and would not take 'no' for an answer. 'I am really jealous of you, Michael,' he told me. 'You have sat with these people in their headquarters, and that is something I have always wanted to do. Sit down and talk with them.'

I told him, 'I think you have a highly romanticized concept of meeting with them. The reality is very different. It is scary and dangerous.'

I believe he sincerely saw himself as a sort of Lancelot, a knight in shining armour, who could perhaps bring all sides together and seek to resolve their differences. His primary motivation was, I trust, full of good intentions – although fraught with perilous consequences.

Despite my better judgement, he pestered me for weeks until finally I agreed to try and set up a meeting for him for the beginning of November. Martin McGuinness agreed to meet

Alan and he became very excited. However, he had only rejoined the Commons as an MP for five months and I am sure that his Constituency Party in Kensington and Chelsea would have deselected him in an instant if they learned he had engineered a private meeting with a representative of Sinn Féin – especially in the company of a Catholic priest who was suspected of being in cahoots with the Republicans.

He must have come to his senses at some stage or sought someone else's advice – someone with official responsibilities that is – because at 6.30am on the day we were due to fly to Belfast, he telephoned and cancelled the visit, even though he had purchased the tickets for travel. He was sorely disappointed but I firmly believed, as I still do, that it was for the best. And of course, it is with great joy in my heart to write that peace has endured largely for some considerable time in Ireland and one can only hope that the dreadful murders early in 2009 will not derail the train of peace which continues to steam through the island of Ireland.

Alan could turn up and make a speech in the House of Commons when he was a little spiritual, and get away with it, and he could seduce the wife and two daughters of a High Court Judge and not be horsewhipped – but I don't think even Alan could have escaped retribution if he had taken tea with Martin McGuinness at that time.

On the day of the first New Labour Budget Speech in 1997, Alan arranged a different kind of tea party, for just the two of us in the House of Commons cafeteria. We were the only two there. 'I don't want to be in the Chamber for all of this,' he told me. 'It will all be lies.'

In the cafeteria you have to collect your food and drinks from the buffet counter and pay at the end – but that didn't suit Alan at all. The Pugin Room was closed because of the Budget Speech and Alan asked the waitress in the cafeteria if she would do him a 'Pugin tea for two'. 'No I can't, ducks,' she told him. 'In here you do it yourself.'

'I can't cope with all that, you'll have to organize it, Michael,' he said abstractedly. I ended up carrying my bag in one hand and a tray laden with tea and cakes balanced on the other. Alan carried nothing.

'We'll go to the terrace,' he said. 'It's much nicer out there.' And he marched ahead leaving me to struggle with my load. We spent about an hour-and-a-half talking about the Church and the Pope when others started to drift out after the Budget speech. But he wasn't interested in the details. 'Much too boring,' he groaned, 'and all lies too! That chap Brown: what does he know about money? As a Chancellor of the Exchequer he makes a damned good second-hand car salesman.' Then he was off with barely a good bye.

In June 1999, Alan had undergone surgery to remove a brain tumour which had nearly killed him – and went to Scotland to recuperate. At the same time, Father Norman Brown, the blind priest, who was chaplain of the Cathedral's Guild of the Blessed Sacrament, was planning the finishing touches to their annual outing. At my suggestion, it was to be to Saltwood Castle and the July date had been set six months earlier for some fifty pilgrims. Alan had proposed we have a special Mass, in the garden by the Castle's chapel ruins, in the names of the four knights who had stayed there on their way to kill Thomas Beckett, the Archbishop of Canterbury.

Though he was still very ill, Alan turned up for the Mass in a white Panama hat – having returned from his stay on his estate in Scotland. The Mass seemed to make him very happy, but any hope this brought me that he might be recovering from his illness was dashed by Margaret McKerow, a doctor with our party, who told me, 'Michael, he has very little time to live.' I was shocked because I had thought the worst was over but was slightly cheered when he told me that our tête-à-tête lunch, which we had planned for while the Guild members visited Hythe, was still on. Jane had arranged for the two of us to have a cold salad in the parlour. We were left alone in the nice, old, wood-panelled room for nearly two hours. Alan told me straight away that he had decided not to continue with his chemotherapy and other hospital treatments. 'I spoke with God while I was in Scotland,' he told me. 'And now I feel utterly at peace.'

Alan told me that one day he had taken a long walk to the top of the tallest hill on his Scottish estate where he had met with God. That is where, he said, he experienced total peace. After talking to God he was no longer afraid to die. He had always intended for himself, and hopefully his family, to be received into the Catholic Church on his estate in September that year.

On the morning of Sunday, 4th September, Jane, his wife of four decades, telephoned me. Caroline Jane Beuttler was thirteen when Clark first met her. They married in 1958; he was thirty, she was sixteen. They semi-eloped and Clark insisted she take a sixteen-year-old school pal with them on honeymoon to keep her company.

This saintly and long-suffering woman, to whom he had been Casanova sinner rather than saint, but to whom he was utterly

149

devoted, told me she thought Alan was near the end. I dropped everything and went to him, getting to Saltwood Castle at about one o'clock. Alan's two sons, James and Andrew with wife Sarah, were there already. Eventually we went up to Alan's bedroom and he was scarcely breathing.

Alan died the next day on the 5th September. Although news of his death was not given to the media until a few days after his death, the reporting was dominated by speculation as to whether Alan had become a Catholic before he died. It was a very difficult time for all concerned and sadly Fleet Street did not cover itself in glory on that occasion. The full story will of course remain known only to Alan and our creator, God. This debate caused a great deal of pain to the family – Jane has always denied that Alan had converted – and to me too, so it was with great relief when I was invited in February 2000 to St Margaret's Church, Westminster, for Alan's Memorial Service.

I arrived as late as I could, with a close friend, Methodist Minister, the Reverend Paul Hulme, and went in through a side door so I wouldn't run into the family. We sat at the back and as soon as the service ended we dashed away through the same side door. A piper outside played a lament from the film *Braveheart,* and I knew that Alan would have loved it. Indeed, and other than, perhaps, St Augustine, a braver heart I have yet to know.

NINE

BUTLINS WITH THE BISHOP– A NAKED
LADY ARSONIST – BAKING MOTHER IN A CAKE –
CRUCIFIXION CENSORED FOR BAD LANGUAGE –
SHOOTING DOWN THE FLOATING CONDOMS –
MURPH THE SMURF, THE CAVIAR-LOVING PRIEST

Westminster Cathedral with its kaleidoscopic silhouette of balconies, tower and domes, almost unique in London for its Byzantine style of the eastern Roman Empire, was my workplace for twenty-four years, twenty of them as ecumenical advisor to two cardinals.

The Cathedral first opened its doors to the public in 1903, fifty-three years after the Restoration of the Hierarchy of the Catholic Church in Britain, and is today visited by countless thousands of worshippers and tourists each week. It is also home to the thirty children who comprise the Westminster Cathedral Choir, not to mention their matron and housemasters, and during the day and night is attended by a workforce of clerics and lay staff and around 500 day students at the Choir and St Vincent Primary Schools. It is the spiritual home of English Roman Catholics and the actual home, in Archbishop's House, of their leader, the Archbishop of Westminster.

I have known it – and loved it – through tears and laughter, anguish and joy, through defeats and triumphs, hope and despair and found its peace and spirituality a healing if not a total remedy for most conditions. And as in most large workforces we have our comedians and grouches, optimists and pessimists, the good and the truly irritating and form friendships and squabble like any other group of workers. Being clerics makes us no different to anyone else. We are, above all, only human...

I suppose that like many large public buildings, a cathedral attracts its share of peculiar and regular visitors. Westminster is no exception. One of the more persistent of these was the woman the Chaplains affectionately named 'Curlers' – because she was never seen out of them, and we never did discover her real name. Curlers was believed to have been a civil servant. She would usually be accompanied by a small trolley and carried a large stick. No-one ever managed to find out what she kept in the trolley, if anything, as it was always covered. She was invariably dressed as a St Trinian's schoolgirl and had a little white face with rouge on her cheeks and a little French beret atop her curlers.

Her favourite pastime was to lay out flat on the floor in various locations in the Cathedral, though she tended to favour the chapels, most often St Gregory's, where Cardinal Hume's body is interred. Some of the chapels are tiny and she usually chose to lie in the doorway, blocking the entrance for other visitors.

Naturally some of the other visitors who had not encountered her before would be concerned – believing she might be ill or even dead, and try to move her or ask her if she was feeling alright. That's when she would leap up and go into battle. On one occasion, she took out a large pair of scissors from her bag and cut a clump of hair from one poor man's head. Usually, when security was called, she would go quietly – but not so if Father Brown was involved.

Father Brown, who had been blind from the very beginning of his priesthood, could only see blurred shapes, even in strong light, but had a great sense of presence, as many blind people do. Father Brown would go around the chapels with his white stick tapping, and suddenly, he would find himself prodding Curlers who was lying on the floor. She could become quite vicious if moved, or in his case prodded, and she would always lay into him with her own stick.

He of course had his white stick but couldn't see her and would take to waving it in front of him to try and protect himself. Willie, the verger, or a passing priest, had to go to his aid on several occasions and everyone breathed a collective sigh of relief when, in the late eighties, Curlers disappeared – probably having decided to move on to another church.

Another regular lady visitor back in the eighties was nicknamed 'The Empire Loyalist'. She was a very majestic lady with a grand imperious voice, like Margaret Rutherford. She would stand in front of the statue of Our Lady of Westminster and shout 'God, save us from the evil toad, Wilson' – this was ten years after Harold Wilson had resigned as Prime Minister. She would do this sometimes several times a day, even during Mass, and had been doing it for years when I arrived. But again she suddenly disappeared in the late eighties and we saw no more of her.

Not so another of our peculiar lady visitors. We saw far too much of her. This particular one would tear off her clothes and run around naked during evening prayer. It may have even contributed to slightly larger congregations in the evening, as word got around, but she was finally barred from the Cathedral after trying to burn me out of a confessional box.

I was sitting inside, hearing confession from a lady, when a lighted candle sailed through the open top of the box and landed in my lap. I brushed it to the floor and stamped it out just as another lighted candle descended, followed seconds later by a pair of them. One must have landed next door because the lady making her confession suddenly yelled, 'We're under attack here.'

When I went outside I found the naked lady, with a fistful of burning candles, which she had been lobbing into the confessional box. With the help of a verger, I managed to defuse the situation, by blowing out the candles she was holding and ejecting her. I never did discover why she wanted to burn me out.

One lady even came to confession with a pet duck in a pram and there was also a very grand lady, who boasted of having sheep and a shepherd to guide them backwards and forwards before her penthouse window in a rooftop meadow in Mayfair. She liked to hear them 'baaa'!

Another lady created a problem after she had baked her mother's ashes into a cake. A local undertaker, Michael, a very theatrical character, called me to explain his quandary about the cake. I'm afraid I found it difficult to take his story seriously and told him I hoped she had used self-raising flour; 'That will give it more life,' I said. But he wasn't laughing.

He explained that the daughter was a Catholic, but her mother, in the cake, was an Anglican. The daughter wanted to transfer her mother to a plastic piggy-bank duck and set her afloat on St James's Park Lake.

In that case, I responded, if the cake is Anglican, you had better talk to the Reverend Howard Pennington, the local Church of England curate. So it was left to my friend Howard to work out how to get the ashes out of the cake and into the duck. Eventually, I am told, he succeeded – I never asked how. But to the best of my knowledge there is still a fake plastic duck floating around on St James's Park lake with this lady's mother inside.

During my time at the Cathedral, I managed to organize several 'firsts'. One of these, in 1991, was an exchange of choirs with St Paul's Cathedral. Our choir went to St Paul's and sang Vespers in Latin, and the current St Paul's High Altar received the first incense in its history – there had, of course, been a Catholic Cathedral on the site before the Reformation and before its destruction in the Great Fire of London in 1666.

Then St Paul's Cathedral's Dean, Chapter and Choir came to us and celebrated an Anglican Evensong in Westminster Cathedral. The Anglican vergers accompanied the choir with their special 'wands' – verges – and it was an altogether different service to that which our congregation was used to. There were a few minor whinges but only one person wrote a letter of complaint: Lord Longford. He had been appalled to attend the Cathedral for what he thought would be Latin Vespers to find

Evensong being conducted by the Dean of St Paul's with their choir singing Anglican hymns and anthems.

'Catholics should expect Catholic services in their places of worship,' he wrote. Not for the first time I found myself completely unsympathetic to one of Frank's grievances.

Though even I was eager to temper another of our inter-faith initiatives which I had helped start in 1992 along with Westminster Abbey's Canon Anthony Harvey (a member of the Harvey sherry family), and the Methodist Central Hall's Dr John Tudor, a Yorkshireman – whom I had nicknamed Friar Tuck because of his impressive girth. It was the Good Friday procession along Victoria Street which we had dubbed 'The Crucifixion on Victoria Street'. In the early years, we used a large group of actors to re-enact the Good Friday story along the way, but eventually it had to stop because of the filthy language used during the actual crucifixion scene. There would have undoubtedly been a lot of abusive language at the time of Our Lord's Crucifixion, but the actors were not shouting the words in Hebrew – they were speaking in English. It might have been just about alright before an exclusively adult audience, but there were thousands of children lining the route and the strong language was far too bad for those young ears. So we dropped the theatrical aspect of the procession and it now takes place each year in silence – perhaps all the more poignant for that.

Another one-off was the centenary celebration in the Cathedral, in June 2003, of the first performance of *The Dream of Gerontius*, the story of a soul going to purgatory, which the composer, Sir Edward Elgar (himself a devout Catholic), had conducted. On this occasion, the Bournemouth Symphony Orchestra performed it again, with the Bach Choir.

Interestingly, the original performance was only allowed in June 1903 because the Cathedral had yet to be consecrated, something which occurred in the July of that year – in those days you couldn't have secular music played in a consecrated place, but the 'law' thankfully was changed some fifty years ago.

The guest of honour at the centennial performance of *The Dream* was The Prince of Wales, who himself had once sung in the London Bach Choir (which rehearses in the Cathedral Hall) and of which he is Patron.

Over the years, the Cathedral has been no stranger to protest. The publication of certain Catholic edicts, or the re-emphasis of traditional Church principles, whether issuing from Rome or from the Cardinal in London, could inflame a passionate response in some people, and incite mob fury in others. We saw our share of both. Sometimes even the most harmless services in the Cathedral would draw the protestors out and have them baying for blood, and though I was obviously aware of certain differences between Churches, I did not think they would react too badly over our special service for Christian Unity, in January 1990. Unity, it was quickly brought home to me, was a dirty word among some Christian Churches.

The annual week of prayer for Christian Unity is held in the week of the 18th to 25th of January, ending for Catholics with the Feast of the Conversion of St Paul, and is now observed all over the world. Cardinal Hume agreed that our special service one year should be the largest ecumenical service Westminster Cathedral had ever attempted. He left me to oversee the arrangements. I invited a number of heads of Churches to speak: Cardinal Hume, of course, and Robert Runcie, the then Archbishop of Canterbury. Other speaking participants were to be Archbishop Gregorios, the head of the Greek Orthodox Church and the Reverend Dr John Newton, Moderator of the Free Churches (unusually from this tradition, one of the greatest scholars on Mary, who spoke on her life). The General of the Salvation Army was present and their International Staff Band played during the service. Chris Patten, the then Environment Secretary, a good friend who lived just around the corner, represented the Government.

The Christian Brethren, a puritan Protestant group, attended for the first time ever and though I invited the Plymouth Brethren and some extreme and obscure groups, few of them wished to be inside – although hundreds of them turned up outside to protest. One or two of their leaders wrote to me saying they would dearly love to take part, but their members would never allow it. There were over two thousand people inside the Cathedral and several hundred chanting protestors in the Piazza.

For what should have been a spiritually uplifting evening for all Christians, there was a great deal of aggression among the mob outside.

After the service there was a reception in Archbishop's House for all the dignitaries, and it was after this that we had to sneak Robert Runcie through the tradesmen's entrance, to avoid the Anglican protestors who were still screaming abuse.

Prior to the event I had been invited to go on a show called *Behind the Headlines* hosted by Jeremy Paxman. There were four guests – me and the late Jim Thompson, then the Bishop of Stepney (who subsequently moved to become Anglican Bishop of

Bath and Wells), Joanna Bogle, a traditionalist Catholic journalist who is a popular writer and speaker, and the Reverend Dr David Samuels, Chairman of the Church Society, a hard line Protestant movement.

So the show started. Joanna Bogle and Dr Samuels were completely aligned at first on policies such as divorce and abortion on which they shared a common view, and were very vociferous. 'Protestantism fits into the English culture like a glove,' said Samuels.

'What did I think?' asked Paxman.

'Well it's obviously a very tight glove,' I said. 'I imagine that Dr Samuels thinks that all Catholics vote in the Italian elections and eat pasta all day. What he should recognize is that we were very much at home here for fifteen hundred years. This is our home; there is no other home. I suggest he gets a new pair of gloves.'

It amused Jeremy Paxman at least, and over the years, stemming from that broadcast, we have become firm friends.

One protest at the Cathedral which did get completely out of hand that year, was led by Peter Tatchell and concerned gay rights. The 29th May 1994 was the official date for the launch of a book called *The New Catechism* on which Pope John Paul II had done a great deal of work, with a large contribution from Cardinal Ratzinger, the current Pope. It was the first major catechism since the Council of Trent in the 16th century.

It was written for bishops and was supposed to make it easier, when passed on, for the laity to understand. There were several points in it, on divorce and remarriage, which didn't please certain factions, and some argued that the Church could have gone further in its compassion towards them.

The group for the ordination of women in the Catholic Church also protested there was nothing in it for them, but the one issue which created anger, protest and even rioting around the world was the section dealing with homosexuality.

It simply reiterated that homosexual activity was wrong, and that was it.

Cardinal Hume had criticized the Vatican for its language on this matter and had wanted to alter some of the words in Latin that were in the text. His Latin was much better than that used in the document. But that was frowned on.

On that Sunday there were hundreds of protestors in the Piazza, many of them dressed in purple, a sign of penance, who were from the group 'Catholic Women for Ordination', and others carrying placards. Most of the protesting factions were orderly and content with making their feelings known outside the Cathedral. But Tatchell, who was leading the gay rights mob, urged them into the Cathedral and right up to the sanctuary – the sacred heart of any church, which contains the altar. There were about a hundred of them, chanting, and they had the Cardinal and clergy surrounded and held up on the sanctuary.

We called for the police, but an age went by and no-one came. Meanwhile our organist, rather humorously and appropriately played, *Dear Lord and Father of mankind, forgive our foolish ways*, like the *Phantom of the Opera*, fantastically loud. No-one could hear anything else so Tatchell's protests were drowned out. This stalemate might have lasted for hours but fortunately one of our vergers spotted a column of mounted riot police, with shields and batons, riding up Victoria Street and asked if they could help. They had come from Parliament Square where there had been a different protest. The officer in charge led the mounted riot police at a trot straight up to the Cathedral steps and with the doors wide open it must have looked to the protestors as if the police were going to charge on horseback all the way up the aisle. Some, looking very fearful, broke away and started making for the exit.

At the last moment the horses were pulled up and, like a cowboy posse, the men dismounted in unison and strode into the Cathedral. Within twenty minutes all the invading protestors had been ejected. But not before they had released hundreds of helium-inflated condoms, some the size of mini airships, ten feet long at least, which floated up into one or other of our five domes.

That was bad enough, but the real problem started when they began to deflate and come down. The first batch descended during the morning Mass, but the majority came down the following evening during a young persons' confirmation by Bishop Patrick O'Donoghue – a steady deluge fell through the readings, the confirmation and finally the Eucharist.

It was difficult for anyone to keep a straight face during the services given that the condoms were drifting down on the congregants' heads. One landed on the Bishop's mitre and he swung out and popped another one with his crozier – his long crooked staff. I doubt that any of those young people will ever forget their confirmation. The final indignity came when one of the shrinking condoms descended on the altar during Mass. What is more dozens of others, whose ends had been more tightly tied off, were still up in the Cathedral's domes and it was thought the farce could last for weeks. The order was received from the Cardinal's office: 'Get rid of the flying condoms!'

The Cathedral always had an ongoing dilemma with pigeons,

which would frequently fly into the Cathedral and be unable to find their way out. Some even tried to nest on the high ledges. They were often removed by shooting them down with air rifles, using special darts, as it was understood to be the most humane method of dealing with the creatures. This method, suggested one of the priests, could also be the answer to the condom problem – and so it was.

One of the Cathedral maintenance men and some of the younger priests set to one evening, after the Cathedral closed at 8pm – and proved to be crack shots, for within an hour every condom had been brought down, some of them exploding with quite a loud bang when they were hit. Those taking part, including myself, held an impromptu drinks party during the shoot-out to celebrate.

The memory of priests, like schoolboys, leaping about the pews, cassocks flying, snapping off rifle shots at huge floating condoms, will stay with me to the end of my days.

It is impossible to write about the Cathedral without saying a little more about one of its most colourful, and larger-than-life, characters – the man known as 'Murph the Smurf', Father Denis Murphy. A self-proclaimed 'first-class snob', with a mischievous grin and a flamboyant personality, he was adored by the parishioners. His love of fine wine and good food was only matched by his zest for living. Top social events around Europe would have been the poorer without his ebullient presence and there was no shortage of benefactors to pick up the bills for his first-class travel and hotels. He always went to the Le Bourget Paris air show by private jet from London and stayed in the ultra luxurious Plaza Athénéé Hotel.

Murph the Smurf was a legendary figure in religious circles and probably the only priest in the world who could correctly identify half a dozen different types of caviar by their taste alone. In keeping with his reputation, Murph's funeral, when it came, was just as unorthodox and hilarious as its much loved star participant. The celebrant was Bishop Patrick O'Donaghue, but the preacher that day was the amazing Scotsman, Father Jim Mallon, who was noted for his unconventional sermons. He did not let us down that day.

As soon as he entered the pulpit he pretended to dial on a telephone and then made the noise of it ringing. 'Pling pling; Pling pling.' Next he pretended to answer it, with the words, 'Hello Denis, is that you?' The entire sermon which followed was an imaginary telephone conversation with the dead priest. 'Who's up there with you? Oh, Basil Hume's settled in well has he? Is Jennifer Paterson doing all the cooking up there? Oh, she's still riding her motorbike – and causing mayhem? Yes, PoD's here, just the same as ever.'

By this time the Bishop was shaking with laughter so much his mitre almost fell off, and the rest of us were giggling like a gaggle of geese. Finally Jim said, 'Perhaps Denis, you will remember this little ditty,' and he began to sing a traditional song of death in Latin. We were already sobbing with laughter, and suddenly the tears were falling in sadness. It was a huge change of mood, from comedy to pathos.

Monsignor George Stack, the then Administrator told him afterwards, 'I always knew you were mad, Jim, but I didn't realize you could sing as well!' What a sendoff for one of our own star performers. Murph the Smurf would have loved it.

As I am sure he and others loved the Cardinal's Christmas Day lunches and other big feasts – which were always very well lubricated and merry affairs. Drinks would be taken before lunch in the Common Room of Cathedral Clergy House before sitting down with the Cardinal for a festive meal that was heavy on food and strong on alcohol. Murph the Smurf frequently dressed as a *Father Ted*-style housekeeper, and would wheel in the flaming Christmas puddings, well-soaked in cognac, curtsy to the Cardinal and make a little speech. Basil Hume loved this part.

This was all followed by coffee and brandies back in the Common Room. At which point most of us would attempt to celebrate Vespers in the Cathedral. Some never made it to the sanctuary, and those of us who did were not completely steady on our feet. On one occasion a priest tumbled and somersaulted his way to the lectern to do a reading and the three celebrants could not remember between them if they had already walked around the altar incensing it, so they attempted it for a second time, but abandoned the attempt halfway round. Merry Christmases indeed! No harm done though, and we always managed to get through it without any <u>major</u> disasters.

TEN

SWINGING LESBIANS – MILES' MISSION – SHOCKING
THE BARONESSES – GETTY – ARUNDEL CASTLE –
CRICKET AND THE ASHES – A SECRET GRAVE
FOR JOHN PAUL

Through my work at Westminster Cathedral, I have been
fortunate in not only meeting some exceptional and famous
people, but also in finding friendship with them – though I must
hastily add, most of them have been rather controversial figures.
They seem to attract me, or, perhaps, I them...

Of all of these, probably none was more controversial, or
eccentric, than Miles Stapleton-Fitzalan-Howard, the 17th Duke
of Norfolk. He succeeded his second cousin Marmaduke to the
main title at the age of fifty-nine, after a distinguished career in
the army, and simultaneously inherited a whole host of lesser
titles. He once quipped, 'I have ten seats in the House of Lords,
and only one bottom to put in them.'

In his first year as Duke, Miles was chiefly responsible for
Basil Hume becoming Archbishop of Westminster in 1976, and
for heading countless charity appeals in aid of the Cathedral,

the Choir School, the homeless centre and the very Church itself in England.

For the last fifteen years of his life – he died in 2002 – Miles Norfolk focused his enormous energies and influence in seeking to uphold what he saw as human dignity, most especially in resisting the efforts of successive Governments progressively to lower the age of consent for gay men and fought three ferocious campaigns to prevent the promotion of homosexuality in schools.

It was the latter of these that caused him to telephone me one evening in 1988. I was out at the time, but on my return I telephoned his London home and spoke to his wonderful, elderly housekeeper. She told me that the Duke was in bed.

'Does he have a cold, or flu or something more serious?' I asked.

'No, nothing like that. He got himself knocked down,' she said, tersely. 'That's what he wants to talk to you about.'

Miles must have assumed that I had already heard the news because as soon as I was put through he began bellowing: 'Bloody lesbians. Everywhere I looked, Seed, bloody lesbians. Swinging from ropes. Knocked me down! Half naked you know?' I thought he had finally gone mad.

'When did all this happen?' I asked.

'Yesterday, in the Chamber,' came the reply. 'They swung down on ropes from the gallery. Knocked me down and damaged my leg. Bloody lesbians!'

It appeared that during the Lords' debate on Section 28 of the Local Government Act 1988, which banned the promotion of homosexuality in schools, three lesbian protestors had abseiled from the public gallery into the chamber of the House of Lords, knocking over several elderly peers, including Miles Norfolk.

Just the thought of him being mown down by swinging lesbians started me giggling and I had to cover the mouthpiece of the telephone with my hand so he wouldn't hear me. After spluttering my condolences and promising to call round and see him the next day, I rang off and collapsed into a chair, overcome with laughter. But I knew the subject was no laughing matter for Miles.

Miles was a charismatic personality with great influence over his fellow peers, and many in the House of Lords were content simply to follow where the Duke chose to lead them. A number of them were often asleep during the debates anyway, but Miles rarely surrendered to boredom and the sandman, and when the division bell sounded, the others would shake themselves awake, look for Miles, and follow him through whichever voting gate he had selected.

On one occasion he did nod off and when the bell sounded marking a vote, he walked through the wrong gate half asleep, and so many others followed him through automatically, and voted for the opposition, that the Tories lost the vote.

From 1998 he became almost obsessed with the 'age of consent debate' and believed it to be his moral duty to prevent it being lowered to sixteen. It was in that context that he called me one day from the House of Lords to invite me to take tea with him. The telephone call alone warned me that this would not be like one of our normal tea-time chats.

'Miles here,' he began as usual. 'I want to talk to you about buggery! Buggery, Michael. Come here for tea and that's what we're going to talk about. All these paedophiles prey on the young ones and we have to protect them. These bloody Labour swine want to make it easier. Hidden agendas there my boy. Make corrupting these children quasi legal. Come at once.'

I hurried over to the House of Lords and found Miles seated at the centre of the Lords' dining room, which was packed. David Hope, then Archbishop of York, was in one corner and other bishops were scattered about the room, including the then Archbishop of Canterbury, George Carey and the Bishop of London, Richard Chartres.

At another table was a large gaggle of Labour Baronesses. Miles had chosen a table near the apex of the L-shaped room, visible to everyone in there.

Walking to the Houses of Parliament, I had thought about the ensuing conversation and had already decided that there was not really much point to it. It was inevitable, with so much Government support, which way the vote would go in the Commons. All the Lords could do, at best, was delay the change in the law, but in the end, they would not prevent it. But this was not an argument worth wasting on Miles in his current crusading posture.

Miles launched into his theme barely before my backside had reached the seat of my chair. 'What are we going to do about these dreadful old buggers? They are obscene!' The Duke was not exactly a quietly spoken man at the best of times, but when his gander was up – and on this day it was definitely hoisted to the limit – he would be almost shouting.

The Baronesses all looked shocked. One even dropped her teacup. Everyone else had stopped speaking. All ears were tuned in our direction.

'So, what does the Catholic Church teach about these old buggers and their unusual practices?' he roared. 'These things go on at school, of course, but normal men grow out of it.'

His greatest concern through this whole period was always that older men could seduce youths at a vulnerable age. Miles was not stupid by any means, and was not a dinosaur. He was a man of the world and a great progressive on controversial sexual issues in the Catholic Church, having given the Cardinal a hard time on the subject of contraception, in which Miles was very much in favour.

I knew, from the continuing silence, that our eavesdroppers were waiting to hear my answer almost as much as the Duke. I didn't want him to explode so I tried the diplomatic approach. I said, 'In his document entitled "Certain matters concerning sexual ethics", Pope Paul VI alludes to the fact that people are actually born that way.'

He blanched. 'You mean the Church condones buggery?' People around us visibly recoiled. It was really rather funny. So much for the diplomatic approach. But I persevered. 'The Church teaches that whether you are heterosexual or homosexual you are not to have sex outside of marriage. But people fail as you know.'

'Then you <u>do</u> mean that the Church condones it.' He was beginning to go red in the face.

'It means, in certain circumstances, it is possible they might not be culpable.'

'You mean they have a licence for buggery in the Church. This is disgraceful.'

Mercifully, the division bell rang out for a preliminary vote for something or other and I was saved from having to continue with the discussion at that time.

During the next three years, the Commons voted on successive occasions for the age of consent to be lowered to sixteen, but each time, and mainly due to Miles's leadership, the Lords rejected the motion. In the end the Government invoked the Parliament Acts, which effectively gives the Commons supremacy over the Lords and in January 2001 the age of homosexual consent was reduced to sixteen. Miles never forgave Tony Blair for pushing that Bill through Parliament.

My meetings with Miles normally took place at the House of Lords or in his London home in Chelsea. But occasionally I would be invited to Arundel Castle, his traditional family seat. The Castle had been saved from the fate of many such homes in the 1950s by the establishment of a family trust, although this did mean that he had to pay £10 per night if he wished to stay there. He sometimes liked to entertain at Arundel and travelled down from London on the train, usually returning the same day. Sometimes he would even leave before his guests had finished lunch. But that was just another of his mild eccentricities.

His lunches were very lavish affairs presided over by himself and his lovely wife Anne. One such lunch, which I attended in 1995, and which was especially grand, was attended by about a dozen guests including the American Ambassador, Admiral Crow, and his wife, the French Ambassador and John Paul Getty and his gorgeous third wife, Victoria Holdsworth.

This first meeting with Getty was particularly exciting for me as I had been in contact with him by letter since the late eighties. I had asked him to support a number of charitable projects and he had generously donated tens of thousands of pounds to those which appealed to him.

We walked together on a guided tour of the castle which Miles insisted on giving us, and ended in the half-Catholic, half-Anglican church where his family's tombs are preserved.

'They won't be able to find me that easily,' muttered Getty. It was a remark I was not to understand until years afterwards.

Getty asked me where I was from and I explained that I was the priest who had been corresponding with him and who had been put in touch by Lorna Gallegos, who was a close friend of his wife, Victoria. We had exchanged letters frequently, I told him. 'Ah, Father Seed,' he said, 'I remember your letters.'

'I just want to thank you for being so generous,' I replied, 'and to apologize to you for pestering you so often.'

'No, Father,' he said gravely, 'keep pestering.'

We talked for a long time about my stay in America and his museum there and he told me I would have to visit him at Wormsley Park, his estate near Henley-on-Thames. We continued to exchange letters and I carried on pestering him to support a number of charities – which he did. Sometimes, when he was in London, I would be invited to his home, at the back of the Ritz Hotel, and over the ensuing years we became firm friends.

He helped with many of my charitable endeavours and on one occasion I mentioned the suffering and atrocities I had seen during a visit to the Balkans. I asked him for his help with aid for the orphans and the destitute there, launched by the Vatican. His response was immediate and generous.

So when I told him, one day, that the Papal Nuncio (Ambassador) to Serbia, Archbishop Eugenio Sbarbaro, an

Italian, was in London, I wasn't surprised when Getty said he would like to meet him, and invited us both to Wormsley for lunch, sending a chauffeur-driven limousine to collect us.

Wormsley is an Elizabethan mansion built of brick and stone in the manner of Hampton Court and is set in thousands of acres of lush parkland – with one unique feature: a cricket ground, styled on, and the same size as, the Oval. Getty had been turned on to the 'national game' by his good friend, Mick Jagger, who is an avid cricket fan, and he had become a fascinated and ardent cricket supporter. It was a passion he shared with Miles Norfolk, who also had a large private cricket ground on his estate in Arundel.

The Nuncio took a beautiful rosary with him as a gift and Getty was extremely touched by his thoughtfulness. For much of our visit the two men talked about the situation in the Balkans and the plight of the orphans there. It was a quiet and friendly and very informal lunch held in a small and intimate dining room and not in the great banqueting hall. John Paul Getty was already in the grip of cancer, but tried to brush it off as being of little consequence, though I knew Victoria was deeply concerned.

Another time, as it approached Ash Wednesday, when we give out ashes, I joked with him about receiving them. I told him I couldn't think of anyone more appropriate, as he loved cricket so much. He relished the idea and I took ashes to his home in London. I presented him with the ashes and then gave him the Sacrament for the Sick and Holy Communion.

Getty craved normality though never achieved it. How could he, coming from one of the world's richest families? He had squandered twenty years of his life in a drug-filled cloud, which almost cost him his sanity and did cost him his beloved second wife Tabitha Pol, who died of a heroin overdose in Italy in 1971. They had one son, whose name probably owes much to the drugs they were taking – Tara Gabriel Galaxy Gramophone Getty.

John Paul Getty fled to London after Tabitha's overdose, fearing arrest, and was disowned by his father. After thirteen reclusive years, holed up in a large house in Cheyne Walk, Getty checked in to the London clinic, at £500 a day for 500 days, to end his various addictions. Getty claimed that the London Clinic did its job, but the person he credited with saving him from destruction was his third wife, Victoria. She had cared for him for twenty years when they married in 1994.

Thereafter he transformed himself into the quintessential Englishman, complete with knighthood and stately home, and in 1997 became a British citizen, entitling him to use his title: Sir. He gave £20 million to the British Film Institute and £50 million to the National Gallery and millions more to individual charities.

Getty was a great admirer of the British military, particularly the SAS, to whom he became a generous benefactor, and he was a regular visitor to their headquarters in Hereford. On one occasion a Benedictine monk from Belmont Abbey in Hereford, Father Thomas Reagan, wrote to me asking if I could help raise funds to build a church and a school. I sent the request on to Getty and when I didn't receive an answer, assumed the project was not to his liking. Two years later, when I had forgotten all about it, I learned he had built the church and school and attended the dedication, flying in by helicopter. Never any publicity of course; not even a word to me.

The end for Getty, when it came, came quickly, and I suppose his tumultuous early life was much to blame. He was 70. Victoria had called me from the London Clinic and he died there in great peace. I anointed him with holy oil and said prayers with her. Getty had been brought up by Jesuits and was a very devout Catholic, having converted as a young man. He died on Holy Thursday – the day before Good Friday – in 2003.

There had already been a meeting in London to discuss the funeral and everyone involved had to sign an agreement not to talk about the details of the arrangement. This was a condition demanded by Getty himself, before he died. He wanted only close family and named friends to know the exact location of where he was buried. Finally I understood the cryptic remark that he made in Arundel Castle.

When I saw John Paul next he was laid out with all his family around him. The rosary, given by the Papal Nuncio, was in his hand and a prayer book was beside him. The Requiem Mass, the following week, carried out by myself and another priest, according to Getty's own instructions, was a moving and emotional experience for everyone present.

The exact details of the service and its location remain a secret.

ELEVEN

DRUNK IN COURT – AN ADDICTION TO GAMBLING
– EX-WIVES BOYCOTT A FUNERAL – 'ON THE MAKE
AND ON THE TAKE' – FINAL TRIBUTE TO 'THE
SILVER FOX'

George Alfred Carman QC, known as the world's most feared lawyer, was just five feet three inches tall, but when you put him in a court room he became a giant.

He married, and was divorced, by three women, whom he battered and abused when he returned home drunk – which was a frequent event. Not one of them turned up for his funeral. George sometimes arrived, still drunk, in court, the following morning, but was nevertheless able to mesmerize the jury with his oratory genius. He rarely lost a case in his career and legal opponents were terrified of him.

He was the truly brilliant – but damningly flawed – star of his profession.

But even taking into account his hopeless addiction to gambling and an irremediable drinking problem – which perversely made him more human – 'Gorgeous George' or 'The

Silver Fox', as he was dubbed, was still head and shoulders above the rest of them, however diminutive he was in reality.

He may have been a celebrity and a household name but only a handful of people attended his funeral in the Lady Chapel in Westminster Cathedral, and not an ex wife among them.

The few included his last close female companion, barrister Karen Phillipps, a fine lady who he loved deeply, and his only child, Dominic with his wife. He was buried in the Catholic cemetery of St Mary's, Kensal Rise, later the same day.

I got to know him well during the last few years of his life, and counted him as a good friend, though he would sometimes cross-examine me in his most ferocious courtroom manner to provide proof of the existence of God, and I found myself frequently feeling sympathy for some of his victims in the witness box. In the end though it was simply fear of the unknown road ahead which made him seek the comfort of an actual, eternal God.

He was sometimes openly aggressive and cuttingly abusive but would confound me by switching, in a flash, to being humorous and human and fun. A quite amazing man, and one whom I liked very much.

George told me that he had himself wanted to become a priest when he was sixteen and had entered a seminary, Upholland, in Lancashire – only to discover, almost immediately, that he liked women too much to swear celibacy for life. So instead he became a barrister and was so unsuccessful that he had to sell first his wife's jewellery, and then their home, to keep going, eventually playing a piano in a pub to pay for food.

But after his dazzling Old Bailey defence of Liberal leader, Jeremy Thorpe, on a murder charge – winning a scarcely credible 'not guilty' verdict – he quickly became the most celebrated lawyer in Britain, regularly earning more than £1 million a year.

I learned that many of his cases were actually won without him even having to put in an appearance. When solicitors had a client facing serious civil charges – for a fee of two thousand pounds he would allow them to use his name, as their proposed counsel, in a letter to the opposition solicitors, to 'frighten them off'. Merely believing that they were going up against the redoubtable George Carman was often enough to make them capitulate and settle. He didn't even know what most of those cases were about, George admitted.

Not that any of these payments gave him much pleasure. They would be frittered away across London's gaming tables in minutes, as fuel for George's gambling addiction. He told me he had squandered millions over his lifetime, but was quite shameless about his twin adherence to gambling and alcohol.

Towards the end of his life this man who was responsible for thirty years of entertaining courtroom drama was often preoccupied with minor problems rather than with headline-grabbing cases. In the winter before he died, in 2000, he was particularly concerned about his senior citizen's heating allowance. 'I've received this money from the Government to pay for my heating,' he said. 'I don't think I should have it and don't want it. I want to give it away.' So I suggested he give it to The Passage charity for the homeless, which he did.

George was famous for his last words to a jury in his summing up at trials. Usually they would be words that would rhyme – so the jury could not easily forget them. Neil Hamilton famously lost his case when George ended his oration with the memorable words, that he was 'on the make and on the take'.

But his last words to me when I spent a final evening with him, at the Howard Hotel, one of his favourite haunts, were of contempt diluted with humour, and were so typically George. We had dinner together and he was looking extremely ill, though mentally alert as ever.

'Did you know, Michael, that two political parties want me to take a peerage?' he asked. 'For some reason they both believe I could do them some good in the Lords. Madness, of course. I'm really not at all keen. What makes them both think I want to be part of them after I have spent a lifetime putting some of their most cherished followers behind bars?

'Become a Lord; I'm not that bored!'

My lasting memory of him will be of his handsome face creased with laughter, an image I carried with me into the Lady Chapel where I celebrated his funeral Mass.

Later there was an enormous memorial for George which Cherie Blair and her close friend, the then Lord Chancellor, Derry Irvine, and a host of other grand people, attended.

But for me, there was the much more beautiful gathering in St Mary's churchyard, when a few of us returned to the grave, for me to bless the headstone which Karen had selected, and had inscribed. There were only Karen, George's good friend, Norman Lamont, and the barrister's teenage grandson to witness this final tribute to 'The Silver Fox.' I could almost hear him chuckling.

TWELVE

ARMY TO THE RESCUE – THE QUEEN CHIPS IN – MAGGIE GLIDES PAST SECURITY – PRINCE ANDREW LEFT IN THE COLD – A FIFTY-FOOT FLYING CROSS – 'VANDAL' MONKS

Erecting a giant, fifty-foot tall, four-and-a-half ton cross in the Cathedral Piazza was never going to be an easy job, and when the Cardinal sanctioned my idea, I turned immediately to my friend General Sir Charles Guthrie, then chief of the UK's Defence Staff and our most senior soldier. Let military might come to the rescue, I thought.

Hume's idea for a symbol in London for the Jubilee 2000 had been that of a crib, but when I suggested a cross he agreed it was more suitable.

I wrote to Sir Charles, outlining the challenge of erecting a cross and he invited me to meet him, face-to-face, in his Whitehall office. He was a convert to Catholicism and keen to help in any way he could. The fact that it was St David's Day and he was an officer in the Welsh Guards also seemed like a good omen.

179

Three uniformed officers, a soldier, a sailor and an airman, were standing to attention outside his door when I arrived, and inside I found Sir Charles, a textbook British general, resplendent in immaculate army uniform, highly polished shoes and spectacles, and with a wonderful, aristocratic accent.

'This,' he announced immediately, 'is probably a job for the Royal Engineers.' Then he called in the army chap who had been waiting outside. The newcomer was full of enthusiasm for the project and quickly concurred with the General that the Royal Engineers were best suited for the job. 'A couple of long, flat loaders and about half a platoon of men and you'll be taken care of,' he assured me. And that, Charles probably thought, was an end to the matter. But I had another idea up my sleeve.

'What about the RAF? It might be easier, and much faster, to fly the thing in by helicopter,' I said.

'Well this fellow will tell us how,' said the General. This fellow, the RAF officer, turned out to be a highly experienced helicopter pilot, who told his ultimate boss that it was crazy to even suggest it. 'It can't be done,' he said. 'Far too dangerous. It would all end in disaster. With that load, the slightest breeze would affect you and the main blades would be bound to strike the surrounding walls or windows.' Just to make the point clear, he said, 'It would crash,' adding for good measure, 'and probably burst into flames.'

Sir Charles was obviously piqued that my idea had been so comprehensively rejected and waved the RAF officer away. Half smiling, and on his way out, the Officer asked, 'Sir, shall I send in the Navy?'

'No, dammit,' said Guthrie, grinning, 'unless Victoria is

expecting to be submerged under ten feet of water in the near future you can tell the Navy to stand down.'

We agreed a fee which the army would charge to transport and assemble the cross, and I left with a note of the name of an officer in the Royal Engineers in my pocket.

A young chap was assigned to the project and he and about twenty-five of his men arrived at the Cathedral on November 24th and set up a tent village in the Choir School playground, including a field kitchen. Some of them stayed in the basement of Cathedral Clergy House and our female staff seemed very disposed to having half-naked young soldiers dashing in and out of the showers and bathrooms. There were grins on some faces on which I had not seen a smile for years.

The serious business of assembling the cross began in earnest on Saturday when another party of civilians, who had driven the parts down on two forty-foot trailers, from Dewsbury in Yorkshire (where it was made), unloaded them in the Piazza.

Most of that day was taken up in sorting out the sequence in which the parts would be put together, and that night we all unwound by consuming an enormous number of beers.

Probably down to our construction workers having gone to bed late, and very drunk, the cross looked decidedly wobbly when they finally got it upright the following morning. It had been assembled flat on the ground and then raised into its vertical, or in this case near-vertical, position. The largest cross in Britain – steel on the inside and wood on the outside – looked as unsteady as some of the soldiers had looked the night before.

All-day emergency action on the Monday left it looking highly vulnerable still, with a distinct wobble, and according to security experts a potentially bigger threat to VIP guests than a terrorist attack. The engineers persisted throughout Tuesday, and by night-time had finally managed to straighten the cross and secure it properly in its stepped base. Wednesday was the opening.

Cardinal Hume had known about my meeting with Guthrie and had personally vetted all the plans and drawings before he died. He told me he thought it was 'a bit over the top' but he genuinely liked it, and approved its design. He died a few months later, believing the cross was there to mark the third millennium and two thousand years of Christianity, and never knew it was to become not only the marker for Jubilee 2000, but also his memorial.

Hundreds of people donated towards the cost, including the Queen. She hadn't apparently thought much of the Dome and the Wheel as symbols of the millennium and wanted something to celebrate Christianity, and when she saw our appeal, seeking funds for the cross, I was told she believed it was a fitting symbol. I understand that the Queen wanted to unveil the cross herself – but in the end she had another engagement and her son, the Duke of York, came in her place. Some donations were as small as fifty pence but over £80,000 was raised.

Security for the opening was the tightest at the Cathedral that I can ever recall and in the weeks running up to the ceremony, we had the boss of Scotland Yard's Special Branch and his men and antiterrorist officers with us for what seemed like most of the time. The Yard man initially demanded that we abandon the ceremony in the Piazza and move it into the Cathedral, until I pointed out that several church leaders would be there solely for the purpose of blessing the cross, which was outside – where it was most definitely going to stay – and it would be difficult to sprinkle holy water from a distance of fifty feet.

The security chiefs talked to us for days about where we were going to put all the bodies if a bomb went off. In the end we agreed on the Crypt near the entrance to the Cathedral. This was supposed to be planning for a joyful occasion but with them it was like a preparation for Armageddon!

On the day, dozens of armed protection officers shepherded their charges in and out of the Cathedral, and sharpshooters ringed the Piazza, concealed on rooftops or behind windows in the surrounding buildings. The most visible security check was on the door of Archbishop's House, where over a thousand guests, many of them VIPs, passed through to holding positions inside the House and Cathedral before being guided out to the Piazza for the service of blessing. Two young uniformed policemen and a police woman were controlling the airport-style security system, with a moving belt x-ray scanner, for checking the contents of pockets and handbags, and a metal detecting doorway to vet the people themselves for concealed weapons. Orders were to make no exceptions.

There were countless ambassadors, high commissioners, members of foreign royal families, Church dignitaries, leading politicians and celebrities present and everyone was made to submit to the checks. Or almost everyone. I watched them through with interest. It was far more stringent than any airport check. Ken Livingstone, then Member of Parliament for Brent East had to empty his pockets, as did Edward Heath and the Archbishop of Canterbury. No exceptions at all were made – until the arrival of Margaret Thatcher.

The police asked Baroness Thatcher for her handbag and for Denis to empty his pockets. He paused to comply but she completely ignored the policemen and glided through the metal detector. The buzzer sounded but nobody, it seemed, was prepared to ask her to undergo a body search – or to open that famous handbag. She didn't think they needed to search her – and probably presumed the security was there for her benefit anyway. The only other exception – and not until he protested – was the then Scotland Yard Chief Commissioner, Lord Stevens, who was accompanied by two senior, uniformed police officers. He did not look at all happy when one of the constables asked him to empty his pockets. The young PC had clearly not encountered his Commissioner before. One of his officers asked the young policeman, 'Don't you know who this is?' And then had to tell him when the constable shook his head. You couldn't invent such moments.

Meanwhile, inside, things were not quite as harmonious as one might have expected. Arrangements for where guests should go had been made by the Cathedral's 'Protocol Officer', a well-meaning chap, but not necessarily the brightest, who was a friend of the Cathedral's Administrator, George Stack, who had appointed him (much to the surprise of the other Cathedral Chaplains). The intention had been to segregate the guests into groups where we thought they might get on with one another. But sadly it had not occurred to the Protocol Officer to list the guests alphabetically and it would seem it had not occurred to him or anyone else that most of the guests would arrive at roughly the same time. The scenes were worse than the opening of Heathrow airport's Terminal 5, but at least in Archbishop's House there were no questions about lost baggage.

In the confusion, the Protocol Officer made a huge gaff in sending Baroness Thatcher to a particular room where she found herself seated on a settee, squashed between, on the one side, Ken Livingstone, and on the other, Edward Heath – two of her arch-enemies. Denis was opposite the three of them, grinning slightly, appreciating the irony of the situation. The three politicians looked as though they had been forced to drink lemon juice. Three very unhappy faces.

Fortunately we were soon able to get everybody on the move again, through the Cathedral and out to their places on the Piazza, facing the blood-red cross on its huge, three-stepped base. As soon as The Duke of York arrived, he performed the official unveiling of the plaque at the foot of the cross before being led to a sentry-box-sized shelter which had been specially put there to shield him from the cold wind or rain. But he and I were in for a surprise. Princess Michael of Kent, who had arrived just in advance of Prince Andrew, had asked if special shelter had been made available for royalty, and having been shown Andrew's refuge (by the very same Protocol Officer), immediately commandeered it for herself.

There was only room for one person, and when Andrew came face-to-face with her, Princess Michael just smiled sweetly – and stayed put. Short of ordering the squatter out, there was precious little the Duke could do but spend the rest of the service exposed, standing outside his personal shelter. Though from the look on his face I suspected he was picturing his unwelcome squatter in far worse surroundings

Just over eighteen months later, the cross was again on the move – on its way to Ampleforth where it was to stand as a permanent memorial to Cardinal Hume (despite tremendous opposition from some of the hundred or so monks there). Why didn't they want it? I think it all boiled down to monastery bloody-mindedness. Because the Abbot was in favour, then the monks would almost automatically object.

It is the way of monks in these situations. Like naughty children who never want to do what the head teacher wants. Monks are rebellious by nature. Libertarians.

In the end the then Abbot, Father Timothy Wright, overruled any opposition and accepted the cross. It was a courageous move, but I think he paid the price in 2005, when his fellow monks failed to re-elect him at the end of his eight-year term as Abbot. Father Cuthbert Madden was chosen instead.

After it was moved and reassembled an attempt was made to erect the cross on its designated site using my previous suggestion to General Sir Charles Guthrie – of lowering it into place by helicopter. Thus the Monastery's neighbours were treated to the wondrous sight of a fifty-foot, blood-red cross flying low in the skies above Ampleforth, slung beneath an RAF Chinook helicopter. It was a remarkable sight, and a great effort, but failed as surely as that young officer had predicted to the General over two years before. With no trees near enough to shield them from the wind, they could not stabilize the cross long enough to lower it successfully into its hole. Eventually the attempt was abandoned and the cross was lowered to the ground and left lying horizontally on the grass, near its intended site.

Abbot Timothy was left with little time before the blessing ceremony was to take place on July 28th and decided to call in a local construction company. Cranes and other heavy equipment were needed, and in the end it cost Ampleforth tens of thousands of pounds, I was told. And still it turned out to be a disaster.

When Hume's family and friends and Church dignitaries arrived for the blessing, the area looked like a building site, littered with tractors and other equipment, and with workmen still struggling to complete the installation. For despite all the rush, the job was not completely finished. It was also raining and thoroughly miserable, and the monks had decided to show their disapproval of the project by boycotting the whole ceremony. Only Abbott Wright and a monk helper were present from the monastery – and he was leading the service.

I was standing with Alan Dodd, the man who had designed the cross – and he was staring open-mouthed at his creation when the ceremony began. Not in awe, but in horror.

'Michael, can you tell me what the hell these stupid idiots have done with my cross?' he growled in my ear. Then louder, so that people around us were turning to listen. 'They're worse than tomb raiders. They are vandals!' I couldn't really argue, as, unfortunately, I knew exactly what he was talking about, and had anticipated just such an outburst.

I had spotted it the moment I arrived at Ampleforth and caught sight of the cross. The elaborate, twisting and tortured, sixteen-foot scroll, or titulous, edged with swirling curlicues and barbs, and with Pontius Pilate's inscription, I.N.R.I – meaning 'Jesus of Nazareth, King of the Jews' – had been left off. I had challenged the Abbot on this before the ceremony.

'We don't need it,' was his simple answer.

I told him that Alan Dodd and the people who had paid a lot of money for the scroll, including the Queen, were not going to be very happy that this integral part of the memorial had been arbitrarily scrapped.

'It was far too fussy and complicated for the people around here,' he explained. 'We prefer a straightforward traditional cross and that is exactly what we are going to have.' His, of course, was the final word, and after overruling his monks to ensure the cross even went to Ampleforth – and though I thoroughly disapproved of his stance – I conceded he had the right to do things his way.

It was much harder though to persuade Alan Dodd that the exclusion of its crowning glory from his massive work of art was anything but an act of wanton destruction. He was seething and cursing throughout the ceremony, as was our companion, Colin Amery, a distinguished architect and then Director of the World Monuments Fund. In the 1980s, Colin had been a member of Prince Charles's group on architecture who prompted the Prince's 'carbuncle' criticism of the proposed extension to the National Gallery and who had, more importantly, paid half the cost of making the scroll.

'That man is a vandal, whatever you say,' Dodd declared loudly, pointing at the Abbot. 'The scroll is a central part of the whole work. It has to be included.'

Even though Dodd was still complaining and Colin was looking rebellious, as though he might join in the insult hurling, I thought we were just about through the worst part. Wrong again. One of the local, Anglican, bishops, who was standing behind us, tapped me on the shoulder and asked, 'Is that a strange new theology? I think there is something funny here. There is only one hole on this side of the cross.' I looked carefully, and saw that there was, indeed, only one hole, at the base of the upright, where Christ's feet would have been nailed. The two holes at either end of the crosspiece, where his hands would have been secured – and which were definitely present when the cross stood outside Westminster Cathedral – were missing.

'No,' I told the bishop reluctantly, 'it is not a strange new theology. It's that the crosspiece has been put on back-to-front.' I thought Alan Dodd was going to burst a blood vessel at least, and I couldn't blame him for being angry. Not only had his beautiful scroll been jettisoned, but someone had carelessly reassembled his cross – and made a terrible and inexcusable mistake. 'How difficult is it?' Alan stormed. 'You don't have to be a top theologian to know that Jesus was attached to the cross with three nails. And on top of that, the whole thing is leaning forward and is extremely dangerous.'

After the ceremony Alan was just as outspoken when dealing with the press and named the poor Abbot, Father Timothy Wright, as the chief vandal. But it had not a ha'p'orth of effect on the Abbot, who remained as intractable on the subject as he had been with me earlier. The cross would remain, naked, as it was – though it was straightened and made more secure. Journalists enquiring at the monastery were told that the scroll had been mislaid. No-one knew what had happened to it. Though this is one puzzle that I am able to provide a satisfactory answer to: the scroll is not, and never had been, lost.

In 2005, I went to Ampleforth and was introduced to a monk, Father Edgar, who had been 'taking care of' the scroll. It has been concealed inside his shed for the past seven years. I felt like

Hans Blix, of the United Nations, looking for a weapon of mass destruction. 'People here didn't like the scroll at all,' Father Edgar told me. 'So I was asked to put it in my shed. I do odd jobs around the monastery and keep my tools and spare parts there. Few go in my shed so it was thought this was a safe place to hide the thing. It took several of us to carry it to the shed and everyone knew it wasn't something to talk about.'

And that, I believe, is where the scroll lies to this day.

$\mathcal{T}$HIRTEEN

TWO WEDDINGS AND NEARLY MY
FUNERAL – GUNS AND CAKE: A MAFIA MARRIAGE –
NATASCHA'S WILDLY ROMANTIC WEDDING –
A WUTHERING HEIGHTS STYLE CEREMONY…
BUT A TRAGIC ENDING

One of the most pleasurable aspects of being a priest is the right to marry people – and I have had the joy of tying the knot for dozens of couples worldwide, some of them rich and famous and others just ordinary folk, and I reserve a special place in my prayers for each and every one of them.

But two particularly spring to mind when weddings are mentioned. One was the most romantic wedding I ever performed – which sadly has ended in tragedy – and the other was the wedding of an American to a young woman closely connected to a top Mafia family – at which I almost got myself shot.

I had been introduced to the bridegroom, William, by his grandparents, during a visit to New York City. He was a US lawman who had fallen in love with this really beautiful girl. They asked me if I would conduct the marriage ceremony in

America and I agreed. I didn't realize until after the service that there were unusual elements at the wedding. On one side was a senior US official and about thirty other lawmen and their families, and on the bride's side, unbeknownst to me at the time, were some of the best known Mafia faces from the Big Apple, mostly members of the notorious Colombo family.

It wasn't until the reception started that I discovered virtually every man in the place was armed. Most of them did not take off their jackets and, when I asked a member of Michael's family why they all seemed to prefer to sweat in the early summer sunshine rather than shed their coats, he told me they were all wearing shoulder holsters and didn't want to expose them. This explained why so many of the women were dancing together – it was too hot for the men.

In the wedding Mass I had said, 'Let us offer each other the sign of peace.' I perhaps should have said, 'Let us show each other our pieces.' (This is US slang for handguns.)

I realized then that I had got myself into a scene which properly belonged in *The Godfather*. Time for a drink, I thought. There was a long bar at the side of the room, but this was very crowded. Then I spotted a smaller bar at the back which had only three men sitting at it – and nobody waiting.

Nearby three small groups of men in black suits, who were not drinking, were closely observing anyone who came close. All eyes followed me to the bar. I noticed that when I ordered a whisky the barman seemed very nervous when he served me, but when it came I sat next to one of the men already there and tried to strike up a conversation.

I asked him if he was a member of either of the couple's

families and if he had ever been to London. After a very long pause he answered in cold, unintelligible monosyllables. The others didn't utter a word but eyed me suspiciously.

Then the first man said, 'You ask a lot of questions. Where are you from?' I was saved from a reply by a woman who came up to me and asked me if I would dance. I obliged and we spent the next few minutes twirling around the dance floor, making idle chatter. Occasionally, as I turned in the direction of the bar and my previous interlocutor, I found his cold eyes fixed on me.

His two companions also seemed to find my partner and I of interest, for their eyes too, followed us around the dance floor. When our dance ended, I showed my dancing partner over to a table near the little bar and was grabbed by the bridegroom's grandfather. 'Do you know who you just danced with?' he hissed.

'No,' I replied, mystified.

'She's the wife of the man over there,' he said, pointing towards the man I had spoken to at the bar, who was still staring at me in an unfriendly way.

'Those three are Dons. You don't approach them, and you certainly don't dance with their wives, unless they give you the OK. Capiche?' (Mafia talk for 'do you understand?')

I nodded vigorously.

'Well keep away from him and for God's sake stay away from his wife or you're likely to be shot – and in a room full of firearms all hell could break loose.'

I didn't think it would be much fun for me either, so I stayed as far away from the Don's bar as possible, until it was time to leave – and I definitely accepted no further invitations to dance.

The wedding of beautiful actress, Natascha McElhone, was as different as it is possible to imagine. Certainly the most romantic wedding I ever performed. It was held in a ruined church, atop a small mountain, an hour's drive north of Marseilles, and Natascha was enraptured by it and vowed to marry there after filming *Simply Picasso* with Anthony Hopkins, in which she played the painter's last wife.

This was the church were, in the film, the couple married and Natascha told me she had sworn at the time, 'Whenever, or if ever, I marry this is where I want it to be'. When she fell in love with brilliant facial plastic surgeon, Martin Kelly, and told him her dream location for their wedding, he readily agreed to be married there.

Natascha, daughter of former *Daily Mirror* assistant editor, Mike Taylor, was already a star and making *The Truman Show* when she met Martin. To ultra-rich celebrities, Martin was the plastic surgeon of choice, but he also gave his services free to the poor and needy who required his skills. Seven years ago he joined forces with fellow plastic surgeon, Norman Waterhouse, to set up Facing the World, a charity treating children from poor countries with severe facial deformities.

I met them both a few weeks before the wedding. They had had difficulty finding a priest to go to Marseilles and a mutual friend, Viscount Randal Dunluce, suggested me. We met several times in Notting Hill, where Natascha then lived, and I agreed to marry them.

The church, when we reached it, was at the back of beyond. Perched on a small mountain, it was inaccessible by road and we had to walk up the last, steep leg, lugging with us a chair for the cellist, and followed by a straggling line of choristers from the village below. There was no proper roof on the building, no toilets and no seating.

It was like a bombsite and the only thing on the altar was their marriage paper. It had character to say the least.

Natascha had brought flowers, which she later offered at the statue of the Virgin Mary, and I must admit the setting was wildly romantic in a *Wuthering Heights* sort of way. I do remember, vividly, the eerie, beautiful solo played on the cello. It was haunting and set all our superstitious, alarm nerves a jangling.

Then it was off to an enormous estate, half an hour's drive away, and a reception which lasted into the early hours.

Natascha and Martin went on to have two children, sons, Theo and Otis, who were with her in Hollywood, where she was filming, in May 2008 when tragedy struck. Martin, an energetic, outwardly fit man of only forty-three dropped dead seconds after opening the front door of their London home. It was the day after their tenth wedding anniversary and Natascha was simply devastated.

Added to which she was four months pregnant with their third child, Rex, who was born in October 2008.

The picture I still have of the couple is of them standing in that derelict church on top of the mountain in France, kissing, after I had just made them man and wife. I was convinced at the time that their love would last a lifetime. As I am sure it would have done if his sudden death had not intervened. God's will, not ours, but still a great tragedy nonetheless.

$\mathcal{F}$OURTEEN

THE DUCHESS SEEKS SYMPATHY –
EIGHTY-EIGHT MEN NAMED IN DIVORCE OF THE
CENTURY – DIRTY DUCHESS? NOT ME! – DOWN
AND OUT IN PIMLICO

I first met the delightful and bohemian Margaret, Duchess of Argyll in 1985 at a Monaco National Day party, in South Audley Street. Her beauty was well-preserved and she was still breathtakingly glamorous. I recall she had made a noisy and flamboyant entrance, was dripping in diamonds under her mink stole and had two handsome friends as her entourage, Nicky Armstrong and John Leach – destined to become pals of mine and both of whom I would later receive into the Church.

'Who is this extraordinary person?' I wondered, as she studied the room from under the corner of her pillbox hat. Before I had time to react, I realized she was moving gracefully through the room towards me. I was the only one at the party wearing a dog collar, which is why I assume she singled me out.

'I'm Margaret Argyll and I need your advice,' she said, dismissing her two escorts with a regal bit of hand-waving.

Her problem was not so unusual. It transpired that a young, foreign maid had run up her phone bill by thousands of pounds and the Duchess was refusing to pay it. But what made her story more interesting to me was the candour which followed. She revealed that access to money was not what it once had been. Ten minutes of further chat on a kaleidoscope of diverse topics and I was hooked and landed. Here was a woman who was stimulating and amusing and I wanted to know her better. And get to know her better I did – but not quite in the style of numerous other male acquaintances from an earlier period in her life...

Nonetheless, Margaret Argyll was to be a phenomenon in my life for almost ten years and I would see or speak with her fairly regularly for the rest of her life. She told me candidly most of what there was to know about her truly astonishing past. It appeared life had changed when she nearly died falling forty feet down an elevator shaft. The fall, and resulting bang on the head and nerve damage, had left her devoid of taste and smell – and also made her become much like Queen Gertrude in *Hamlet*, so vividly described by the Danish Prince, with insatiable desires.

After an earlier marriage had ended in divorce, Margaret had set up in a house in Mayfair left to her by her father and entertained some of the big names of the day – Cary Grant, Noël Coward and John Paul Getty were among her house guests, and Lauren Bacall and Deborah Kerr were regular visitors too. In 1951, at the age of thirty-eight, she became the third wife of Douglas Campbell, the 11th Duke of Argyll. They were blissfully happy at the start of their relationship. 'I had it all,' she told me.

'Wealth, beauty and recognition as one of the ten best-dressed women in the world.' Cole Porter even mentions Margaret in the anglicized version of his hit song *You're the Top*.

She was a duchess, was able to call a large, ancient castle her home, and her daughter by her first marriage went on to marry a duke. But Margaret told me she realized she wasn't at all ready to settle into a life of aristocratic grandeur with Douglas Campbell, who she soon found 'boring' and predictable. Her eventual divorce from the Duke was well-publicized and caused much scandal and lurid reporting at the time.

Margaret had embarked on over a hundred affairs during her eight years of marriage to him, claimed the Duke. He named eighty-eight of them in his divorce petition, including three royals and two government ministers. And he produced two famous Polaroid photographs of her 'headless' lovers. Outrageously, Margaret had allowed herself to be photographed nude, apart from a string of pearls, with a naked man, whose torso was shown but not his head, and in another photo she is pictured with another unidentified naked man. The identity of these two men has, I hear, been the subject of endless speculation!

It is now understood that the Polaroid camera, then the only one in Britain, was in the possession of Her Majesty's Government, on loan from America to a member of the Cabinet. It also appears that the other anonymous headless man was a well known American swashbuckling actor. Amazing really, when you think about it, that with this remarkable, technologically-perfect new camera, they consistently managed to take photographs missing off the subjects' heads!

Margaret clearly enjoyed her notoriety and was completely

unrepentant and, moreover, genuinely could not understand how she came by the nickname 'the dirty Duchess'.

In granting the divorce the Judge, Lord Wheatley, said the Duchess had indulged in 'disgusting sexual activities', adding, 'She is a completely promiscuous woman whose sexual appetite could only be satisfied by a number of men,' he said.

To me, when reminiscing, the Duchess always dismissed His Lordship, Judge Wheatley as 'a miserable old codger'.

Before I knew her she had lived in great style, with a butler, in her house at 48 Upper Grosvenor Street, but as the years passed, the free-spending Duchess found her fortune diminishing rapidly and was forced to open her house to the public for paid tours. By 1978 she had to move to a rented apartment in Grosvenor House, Park Lane where she kept the services of a single maid. Her way of life may have plummeted but Margaret never felt sorry for herself and certainly had no regrets about her life. 'Oh, Father Michael,' she would say, with a radiant smile, 'it's all been such marvellous fun.'

But by 1993 she was unable to look after herself independently and her children placed her in a nursing home in St George's Drive in Pimlico, near to the Cathedral. I visited her in her extremely tiny room, where she lived out her life with her pet poodle. It was a far cry from the millionaire's home in New York where she was raised as a cosseted only child, or the vast, historic castle over which she was mistress.

She died in July that year after a bad fall, and I assisted at her funeral, which was fittingly held in the very grand society church, Farm Street, Mayfair, run by the Jesuits. One of her close friends, Larry Adler, played a moving, musical tribute at the Requiem Mass on his harmonica. I suspect several of Margaret's former beaus were in the congregation, as there were a fair number of good looking men, of a certain age, present among the mourners.

And so ended what had been one of the most colourful and eventful lives of the twentieth century.

$\mathscr{F}$IFTEEN

MASTER OF SCHMOOZE - 'LORD CASHPOINT' - DIRTY TRICKS IN THE MEDIA - *THE SOUND OF MUSIC* AND MEDALS

The *Guardian* once described Anthony Bailey as 'one of the most influential men you have never heard of'. He is a consummate go-between, the peerless broker, a friend of many European royals and half the Saudi inner Royal Family, the Chair of the Government's Faith Task Force, and one of the people identified by Labour to help boost their depleted coffers.

In this context, one might think it strange that just three years ago, a personal donation by Anthony, of £500,000, was rejected by the then chief Labour fundraiser, Lord Michael Levy.

Even stranger that, shortly afterwards, with Lord Levy out of the picture, other donations were accepted.

Michael Levy is one of the few men I have encountered who, I don't mind admitting, I found it difficult to warm to. Mainly, it is true, because of his treatment of Anthony Bailey's donation, for which I felt partly responsible, as I had indirectly introduced them, but also because of his bruiser-like persona. He was well known for securing donations by a combination of charm and schmooze.

The life peer dubbed subsequently 'Lord Cashpoint' by the media, was born of poor immigrant Jewish parents in run-down Hackney. His 'rags to riches' transformation came from his management of pop stars, like Alvin Stardust, and the sale of his record label, Magnet, for £10 million in 1984, the year he met Tony Blair. Things became rather difficult for Michael Levy when he found himself at the centre of the 'cash for honours' scandal in 2006 and was one of a number arrested and interviewed by police during their investigation – although in 2007 the Crown Prosecution Service announced he would not be prosecuted. Lord Levy has always maintained that he has done nothing unlawful.

The origins of the debacle were rooted in the Government's City Academies programme first announced by the then Secretary of State for Education, David Blunkett, in 2000. The concept of the Academies was that they were to be all-ability, state-funded places of education established and managed by sponsors from a wide range of backgrounds – including high-performing schools and colleges, universities, individual philanthropists, businesses, the voluntary sector, and the faith communities. The theory went that sponsors could challenge traditional thinking on how schools should be run and what they should be like for students, seeking to make a break with the culture of low aspiration which sadly we know afflict too many communities and their schools.

Seeking to raise educational outcomes for young people from

deprived backgrounds and neighbourhoods is something to be welcomed by all. But where the policy started to unravel was the expectation of some philanthropists to be 'rewarded' for their generosity. All of this was exposed in 2006 when Des Smith, an advisor to the Specialist Schools and Academies Trust – another one to be arrested – revealed what appeared to be a 'tariff system', in which a benefactor who gave to 'one or two' academies might receive a State honour. Hence the 'cash for honours' scenario...

Before all this emerged, I was asked, early in the scheme, if I knew of anyone who might be able to help a particular Catholic school, run by a religious Order of Brothers, in a needy part of south-east London to become an academy. I immediately thought of Anthony Bailey, whom I knew through his interest in heraldry and his inter-faith work. I called him and asked if he, or any of his contacts, might be prepared to help. His answer was an immediate yes.

Within days I accompanied him to 10 Downing Street for a meeting with education chiefs. After that meeting, I had nothing to do with the arrangements going forward. As the years passed, Anthony managed to find several different sponsors for the Academy programme raising more than £8 million to support a number of schools. As I understood it, the gossip in the tearooms at Westminster was that Lord Levy was becoming somewhat rattled by Anthony's successes – and perhaps feared he might be displaced as Labour's chief fundraiser. Anthony was already being called in certain circles 'the new Lord Levy'. I understand the word 'jealousy' was used by some, even those within the Cabinet and officials in Number Ten.

In March 2005, Anthony's reputation took a hammering when it emerged that a £500,000 personal donation to Labour had been returned a month after being accepted, being sent back (with interest), with no specific reason being stated as to why it was being rejected. Rumour circulated that Lord Levy feared the money may have come from foreign businessmen. Anthony insisted the money was his own and that that he was being deliberately smeared by this allegation, and issued legal proceedings against those who stated that it came from overseas.

Then *The Sunday Times* printed an article about Anthony which he found very upsetting. It was an extremely unpleasant episode and became more so when the press then directed their enquiring lens towards me. A story appeared in *The Daily Telegraph* which broke on my fiftieth birthday – which that June I was spending in the country. Anthony telephoned me that evening and read the article to me. It claimed:

'Tony Blair's personal priest, who has taken a vow of poverty, has helped raise millions of pounds for the Prime Minister's flagship City Academies – to the dismay of the Church hierarchy. Introductions by Father Michael Seed, the ecumenical adviser to Cardinal Cormac Murphy-O'Connor, the Archbishop of Westminster, led to at least three supporters being found to back the schools project.

Father Seed, a Franciscan friar – introduced Anthony Bailey, the millionaire public relations executive, to two senior Downing Street officials at a Westminster reception. Mr Bailey, a leading Roman Catholic who is to chair the Government's Faith Task Force when it launches next month, subsequently secured £8 million from three businessmen who have sponsored four academies.

The Daily Telegraph has learnt that Fr Seed's connection to the academies project has caused concern at the most senior levels of the Roman Catholic Church, with Cardinal Murphy-O'Connor privately expressing 'deep unease'.

The Cardinal is unhappy that Fr Seed should have been seen to be involved in helping a project so closely associated with the Prime Minister. The Cardinal has told senior bishops that he feared the introduction could be seen as blurring the boundaries between the Church and party politics. Neither the Cardinal nor Father Seed would comment last night.'

Well I, for one, was never contacted nor given the opportunity to speak, and the Cardinal assured me that none of the comments, or sentiments, contained in *The Daily Telegraph* story, was his.

It appeared to me that someone was trying to create a conspiracy where none existed. I had simply proposed Anthony for the Academies Scheme, and thereafter I had not been involved. I half expected Scotland Yard detectives to come knocking on my door – but I at least was spared that. I subsequently discovered that a senior employee of the Catholic Church's London media office had been briefing journalists, and attributing remarks to the Cardinal without ever consulting him.

Questions were asked in the Commons about any payments to Anthony, but Jim Knight, Minister of State for Schools and Learners, exonerated him in response to questions. He reported that Anthony was on the Governing Bodies of two city Academies but had never received any payment for his work. Subsequently, the Labour Party apologized unreservedly to Anthony for any distress that the affair may have caused.

My first face-to-face meeting with Michael Levy took place about a year after all the debacle. It was, as many of the more eccentric moments of my ministry, in the House of Lords when I happened to be with Lord Alton. Having heard so much about Michael, I was anxious to find out just what kind of a man he was, and the moment presented itself when I was standing by 'Brass Gates' in Peers' Lobby. Michael Levy appeared with a group of guests and caught sight of me talking to David Alton – I was rather distinctive in a brown habit amongst the tide of grey suits – and he immediately scuttled through a set of doors towards the Peers' lavatories, leaving his guests stranded with the saintly doorkeepers as hosts. I asked David if we could wait. And wait we did – as did his guests.

Levy didn't reappear in Peers' Lobby for some considerable time and when he emerged, his head was first to appear from around a door, as he scanned the Lobby seemingly for friends or foe. Much like one of the hit numbers from the musical *South Pacific*, our eyes met across a crowded room – only this time a Lobby – though he seemed a little startled to find us waiting; I had the impression he had hoped we would be gone.

David made the first move. He stepped forward and said, 'Hello, Michael' and introduced me to Lord Levy. It was the first time Lord Alton had ever spoken to Levy. Michael Levy appeared to know who I was, and seemed rather nervous and was not acting at all naturally. His first words were to blurt out that he had given Tony [Blair] a bible. 'That was nice,' I replied.

Then David said, 'Father Seed occasionally does services for the PM at Downing Street.'

'But it's Peter Thompson who really looks after him,' said Levy. Peter was an Anglican priest from Tony's youth who had become a close friend and adviser to the former PM. Lord Levy's statement would have been right when he first met Tony in the early 1980s but the Reverend Peter Thompson had returned to Australia some years before.

David zapped back, 'A bit far for Peter to come, all the way from Victoria, Australia, to do services in Downing Street. I think Father Seed is more conveniently sited in Victoria, London. And you might have forgotten that the Blairs prefer Catholic services?'

With that, Michael Levy was at a loss for words and, conveniently remembering his guests were still loitering in Peers' Lobby, made his excuses and dashed off. That was the last time I saw him.

Through Anthony Bailey's multi-faith work and international relations, he has been the recipient of a number of prestigious foreign decorations and awards. Anthony was for some time the British and Irish Delegate for The Sacred Military Constantinian Order of St George, a Roman Catholic Order of Knighthood which undertakes spiritual, humanitarian, hospitaller and charitable projects and initiatives across Great Britain and its dependant territories, Ireland and the world.

A few years ago, after a particularly successful international trip, Anthony returned to London with a heavy host of foreign honours. After all, medals, sashes, swords, chains, stars, citation parchments and miniatures – not to mention signed, framed photographs of sultans, leaders, potentates and presidents – do have a great weight, especially from the Middle East (with all their precious stones).

Subsequently as a courtesy, and to meet with the rules of protocol, Anthony wrote to the then Private Secretary to Her Majesty (whom he knew) to seek permission to wear the decorations at Court. The ever-patient Sir Robin Janvrin had the onerous task of seeking the Queen's permission. At the beginning of the week and at the end of his daily audience with Her Majesty – once State Papers and other pressing matters had been dealt with – Sir Robin was asked whether there was any other business before the Queen commenced her schedule of engagements for the day. Sir Robin replied, 'Just one thing, Ma'am. His Excellency Anthony Bailey, Delegate for The Sacred Military Constantinian Order of St George, has recently completed some charitable work abroad and the King of Morocco has awarded him the honour of Knight Commander of the Royal Order Al-Alaoui. Mr Bailey has written to seek permission to wear the decoration at Court.' Her Majesty was gracious to agree.

On the Tuesday, the same procedure was followed, but Sir Robin felt he could ask for a little more since he had been successful on the first day. 'Ma'am. His Excellency...' and so it went, 'visited the Republic of Lebanon and has been made a Knight Commander of the National Order of The Cedar. And Ma'am, he also went to the Republic of Yemen and is apparently "First Class with Collar Grade of the Order of Unification".' Her Majesty, keen to press on with engagements, agreed to the wearing of these decorations too.

And so Wednesday came, the same, this time with a gong from Bulgaria – a First Class Order of the Madara Horseman; Thursday and Friday followed with yet more decorations (including from the Syrian Arab Republic) – 'First Class Grade of the Syrian Order of Outstanding Merit' – and from the Portuguese Republic (something he had acquired a little earlier) – a Knight Commander (with Star) of the Order of Infante Dom Henrique. On the Monday of the following week at the end of business with Sir Robin, Her Majesty inquired whether there was any further business. Sir Robin replied, 'No, Ma'am,' to which The Queen rather quizzically responded, 'What? No Mr Bailey today?'

Ironically, when Anthony was subsequently awarded an OBE for services to inter-faith, it was The Prince of Wales who undertook the investiture.

Anthony's joy was made complete in October 2007 when he married Her Serene Highness, Princess Marie Therese von Hohenberg, the great-great-granddaughter of Archduke Franz Ferdinand (whose assassination triggered World War I) at one of the most talked about society weddings of the year at the Arch-Abbey of St Peter in Salzburg, Austria – the venue used in *The Sound of Music* for the wedding of Captain Von Trapp (Christopher Plummer) to Maria (Julie Andrews). The whole thing was utterly glittering...

$\mathscr{S}$IXTEEN

HELL FIRE THREATS FOR BILLY – HUME BACKS THE REVIVAL – A MAN WITH A CRACKLING CHARISMA – 'THE FILTHY PROTESTANTS' – ANGER AND HATRED AT A CHRISTIAN RALLY

It was brave of Cardinal Hume to support American evangelist, Billy Graham's last 'Life' Mission to Britain in 1989, and even braver to attend one of his mass rallies in the face of death threats and vicious abuse.

Billy Graham, who was then seventy and had spent the whole of his life preaching the gospel to 200 million people worldwide, also received death threats for associating with the Catholic Church, and was threatened with everlasting hellfire for consorting with the Antichrist – as we Papists are often referred to.

This was the first time ever that the Catholic Church had formally been involved with one of Graham's missions to Britain since they began in 1954. In the past he had always relied on other churches, mainly evangelical ones, to invite him over – Church of England, Methodists, Baptists or Salvation Army – all had been involved at some stage, for he refused to impose himself on a country without a proper Church invitation.

On this occasion, for reasons best known to him, he had decided to come to Britain only if the Catholic Church extended an invitation, irrespective of the other Churches. Times were changing, thank God!

Cardinal Hume was fully aware that we faced a powerful backlash from certain evangelical fundamentalist Protestants and traditional Catholics if we aligned ourselves with Graham, but he was never afraid of controversy, if the project was worthwhile, and he deemed support of the world's greatest evangelist more than deserving. It was, he said, essential.

When Billy Graham came to visit us at Archbishop's House before the start of his Mission, I was not sure what to expect. I suppose my mental image was that of a rather showy, dazzling individual with more than a touch of show business about him. But the elegant, white-haired man, who had been preaching for over fifty years, was a gracious and charming gentleman who wasn't at all flamboyant – though he was possessed of a potent, crackling charisma. A truly great man.

He had allowed two hours for his visit, but the Cardinal had an emergency meeting that afternoon with Kenneth Baker, the then Secretary of State for Education, and he left me to entertain our guest for the next hour. I had, at very short notice, to find things to show Billy Graham. The Cathedral Choir School seemed the ideal place.

In the School, he enjoyed talking, and swopping jokes with the youngsters, though being very tall he towered over them and peered down through dark glasses – his only affectation, as far as

I could see. Later he was moved to tears by the choristers' rendition of Schubert's *Our Father* in the rehearsal room. Sitting next to him, and later when we knelt together in prayer, in the Cardinal's private chapel, I could feel the power and the passion of the man emanating almost in waves. It was almost as though he was electrically charged.

The next time I saw him was at London's Earl's Court Arena on the second night of his rally there, surrounded by thousands of adoring worshippers and a few hundred potentially dangerous protestors. Because of these protestors we almost didn't make it into the secure parking area. Dozens of them surrounded our car as we approached and began banging on the roof with their fists and screaming abuse through the windows.

Our driver, the Cardinal's then Private Secretary, Monsignor Vincent Brady, was very worried indeed.

As usual, because there was more legroom, the Cardinal was sitting in the front passenger seat and I was in the back, in my friar's habit. Because I was in the back and, therefore, deemed the more important passenger, most of the abuse and rude gestures were aimed at me. 'Whore of Babylon!' screamed the crowds. 'Antichrist! Burn in Hell!'

'Oh, they are giving you a very warm welcome,' I observed to Cardinal Hume.

'The filthy Protestants are really out to get you this time, Michael,' he replied in his drunken Irish voice, which didn't cheer me at all. 'Do you think they're happy to see me?' he asked, in his normal voice.

'Yes. You're the representative of the Devil,' I told him. 'If you're assassinated today it's a wonderful day for strawberries. When you have your Saint's day, on this day, people will be able to have picnics with strawberry teas. Red is good for hiding the blood.'

Finally, a security team reached our car and shepherded us into the safe parking area, though the voices of protest continued unabated. We had joked with each other, which was our standard way of dealing with danger, but there was a lot of anger and hatred out there, focused at us that night.

It wasn't mentioned to our host however, when we finally went inside and were shown to a reception area where Billy Graham, chatting to Cliff Richard, was at the centre of his entourage. After the previous ten minutes of abuse and violence it was almost surreal to be sipping tea with the Cardinal, the world's greatest evangelist and an international pop star. Cliff Richard had first become a committed Christian under an earlier Billy Graham Mission to Britain many years before.

Various members of the Royal Family were there during the week-long Mission, including Princess Margaret. The Queen and her sister were avid admirers of Billy Graham, who always preached privately to the Queen on a Sunday in one of the royal palaces, before or after his Missions.

Cardinal Hume sat in front with Billy Graham's wife, Ruth – who died in 2007 – and the then Bishop of London, Graham Leonard (who shortly after became one of the first Anglican bishops to convert to Catholicism, being Received, and conditionally ordained a priest, by Cardinal Hume himself). His chaplain, Canon John Shepherd, who a few years later I Received into the Church, was with me in the row behind, together with Monsignor Brady.

The two Anglicans were in no way natural allies of Billy Graham; they were seriously High Church, staunch Anglo-Catholics (in reality 'higher' than both Hume and myself). Dr. Graham was far too Protestant for either of them, though they respected his traditional teaching of basic faith. It was quite funny watching them saying their Rosaries and muttering their Hail Marys.

This kind of rally wasn't their style at all, with guitars and songs and all the American razzmatazz.

Throughout the rally, every few moments, someone would stand up in the auditorium and hurl obscenities and accusations of heresy against either Billy Graham, or the Cardinal, or both. The Bishop and his Chaplain looked quite bewildered, though I wondered, mischievously, if they might not be a little in sympathy with the protestors from a reversed point of view!

Still, it is difficult to have anything but admiration for a man who has preached Christianity to live audiences of nearly 215 million people in more than 185 countries and territories and reached hundreds of millions more through television, video, film, and webcasts. Some Pastor!

$\mathcal{S}$EVENTEEN

FOREIGN OFFICE DESIRES TO 'DOWNGRADE' VATICAN – SWORDPLAY WITH RYAN AIR – YOUNGEST AMBASSADOR SAVES THE DAY – PRESIDENT'S FLAG IN SECOND PLACE

In the latter part of 2005, the Foreign and Commonwealth Office (FCO) was believed by many in the Vatican to have either succumbed to a temporary bout of madness or, less credibly, that the Whitehall mandarins had chosen deliberately to insult the newly elected Pope Benedict XVI.

This alarming reaction had been caused by the decision to seek applications for a new British Ambassador to the Holy See by advertising the post in a newspaper. It was the first time one of Her Majesty's Ambassadors had ever been sought through such a process. And the hurt felt was magnified, given that the Mission to the Holy See is Britain's oldest diplomatic posting, established in 1479.

The pundits considered that these changes were, at best, a clear Foreign Office move to downgrade the post of British Ambassador to the Vatican, and when rumours subsequently began to circulate that Britain planned to sell off not just the Ambassador's car, but the embassy and the official residence too (which had huge grounds and was where the Queen had stayed on visits to various Popes), the Catholic Church was, not surprisingly, more outraged. The move had apparently greatly upset those close to the Pope and the Foreign Office's actions were felt to be demeaning.

The FCO, they believed, had started plotting the closure and the downgrading of the ambassadorship six months earlier upon the death of John Paul II and during the subsequent Papal vacancy.

On top of all this, the post was advertised with a salary of only £40,000 – and expenses of just £6,000 a year. A small reception on the Queen's Official Birthday would swallow up the whole annual allowance in one go. The signal apparently being sent to the Vatican was that Britain no longer considered them to be of any significance whatsoever on the world stage.

It was a reasonable assumption, as I was told that some senior Foreign Office officials saw the Vatican ambassador's role as less important than that of Santa Claus in Lapland or a new Mayor for Toytown.

Despite the modest rewards there were over two hundred applicants eager to take on the job of British Ambassador, most of them, I was told by friends in Government, either extremely suspect or undesirable characters, or just plain crackpots.

But the Foreign Office mandarins were not unduly concerned as they had already earmarked one person for the job, someone who was rich and who owned a large property in Rome and who was prepared to put a Union flag above it and use their own money to subsidize the British Government. To this person, backed by senior politicians and influential Foreign Office bigwigs, the post was of glamour-interest only; the appointment was considered by many to be a *fait accompli*.

Fortunately for the Vatican – but not it seemed for many in the Foreign Office – the successful applicant for the vacant post was a young Irishman, who made history by becoming the first Catholic envoy to the Pope since the Reformation. Some very senior people had monitored the interviews and convincingly axed the mandarins' shoo-in choice.

The young man in question was Francis Campbell, a civil servant, who had been Tony Blair's Secretary for Foreign Affairs, and later Private Secretary, and had spent a total of four years in Number 10 Downing Street. He is warm and friendly and is well liked by both Tony and Cherie Blair. They deeply respected his straightforward, no-nonsense advice and natural charm.

It was an opinion not initially shared by some of Jack Straw's – then Foreign Secretary – cohorts at the Foreign Office. Francis Campbell had followed his stint in Downing Street with two years in Rome as First Secretary in the British Embassy, and later as Senior Policy Director of Amnesty International. A man of integrity, he resigned after just days over their policy on abortion had been announced. He spoke both French and Italian well.

The last thing the Foreign Office had wanted was an experienced diplomat with the ear of Downing Street. But they still had a few tricks up their sleeves. If the Vatican had been puzzled and angered by Foreign Office actions to date, they were about to become even more bewildered and troubled by the British Government's next moves.

Britain's new Ambassador to the Holy See, at thirty-five the youngest British Ambassador in the world, arrived in Rome in December 2005 on a one-penny ticket issued by Ryan Air, having paid his own fare. With him he carried his full regalia, which he would wear in presenting his credentials to Pope Benedict, including his ceremonial sword. Except that Ryan Air would not allow this very dangerous item on board their aircraft. Not even, it seemed, in their hold. Francis argued; Ryan Air stood firm.

In the end it had to be sent, accompanied by an official flunky, on British Airways, the airline normally used by the Foreign Office, where ambassadors always fly Business Class, and at a fare considerably higher than that paid by the sword's new owner.

In Rome, Francis discovered he still had an official residence, Villa Drusiana near the Appian Way, but only just. The rumours that he was about to lose his Embassy, residence and official car could not have been more accurate. No staff remained in the villa and he was totally alone in the huge house. The British Embassy to the Vatican on Via Condotti was already abandoned and its reduced staff complement were working out of the British Embassy to Italy. The ambassadorial car had been sold.

It seemed that the Foreign Office were quite prepared to see Francis, in full regalia, make his first trip to meet the Pope on the notorious 64 bus, on which his sword would probably have been stolen, or a hired taxi. But the British Ambassador to Italy, Sir Ivor Roberts, avoided what would have been the nation's embarrassment by offering his own limousine and chauffeur.

In January, as Francis was moving from the Villa Drusiana to a temporary residence, the Pope's Secretary of State, his equivalent of Prime Minister, Cardinal Angelo Sodano, let Jack Straw know that His Holiness had had enough. The 'White One' as he is known by the clergy, was, like Queen Victoria, not amused. Sodano warned the then Foreign Secretary that Britain risked violating a long-standing treaty by moving our Vatican Embassy to the same premises as the British Embassy to Italy. The Vatican has Sovereign Status and thus is entitled to a foreign mission separate from Italy. It was the first major row between the two countries since diplomatic relations, which had been broken off in 1534, were re-established in 1914 – initially with a humble Mission and without an ambassador.

If the Foreign Office mandarins had hoped for a quiet merger which might go unnoticed or condoned by Vatican officials, they were to be seriously disappointed. The resented snub to the Pope in advertising for an Ambassador to the Holy See had concentrated the international Catholic Church's focus on the Embassy.

As a team from the Foreign Office flew in to Rome to try and head off a full scale diplomatic row, Francis Campbell himself solved the problem. He found a cheap, quite large apartment, on the top floor of the Palazzo Pallavicini. Probably originally intended as servants' quarters, these rooms were quite suitable for his needs and gave access to a large flat roof area where a few dozen guests could be entertained if necessary. Maybe not suitable for the Queen or Prime Minister to stay in, as they had in the previous residence, but more than enough to satisfy our humble and easy going ambassador. He also managed to negotiate space for the Embassy in Via XX Settembre, and the crisis was over. Since then, I believe, Francis has done a brilliant job in re-cementing relations with the Vatican.

Except that he has told me he currently has one small problem. The Union flag, which is somewhat worn and flutters from a makeshift flagpole above Francis's aerie, has provoked a complaint from the Italian Government. It seems it is flying slightly higher than the Italian President's flag just across the road. Serves them right for invading Britain in 43 AD and staying 400 years!

They want it lowered a bit in deference to their leader, and have now made the request on more than one occasion. To date though it is still up there and I know that His Excellency the Ambassador would appreciate someone donating a brand new Union flag and a decent flagpole.

To push it just that little bit higher!!

$\mathscr{E}$IGHTEEN

ALCOHOL FLOWS AT SANDHURST – CADETS LET
OFF STEAM – MY VALUES OF TEMPERANCE SPEECH –
HOW PIERS MORGAN MISJUDGED THE MOOD

The first time I went to the Royal Military Academy at Sandhurst, I was mistaken for the Permanent Under-Secretary of State for Defence, the late Sir Michael Quinlan, who was my host. He was the top civil servant for the armed forces and a brilliant after-dinner speaker.

For ten years, from 1990, I 'looked after' Wellington Barracks as Officiating Chaplain to the Forces, a not unusual occurrence, as there are sadly just not enough full time Catholic priests in the services to go round. One of the fringe benefits from this arrangement was that I found myself invited to many of the army's social functions, and discovered that as well as being the best fighting men in the world, our troops also have, and justifiably so, the finest reputation on earth for partying – one such memorable event being the annual 'Campion Dinner' for Catholic cadets and their friends at Sandhurst.

Edmund Campion was an English Saint who illegally ministered to Catholics under Elizabeth I, and was held in the Tower before suffering the horrifying martyr's death of being hung, drawn and quartered at Tyburn at the age of forty-one.

In November 1991, Sir Michael and I were driven from Westminster to the Officer Training College in a government car. After excusing himself, Sir Michael spent the whole journey working his way through his Permanent Secretary's Black Box filled with documents marked 'Top Secret'. I was tempted to have a glance but occupied my time saying the Rosary.

At the gated entrance to Sandhurst there was high security and soldiers checked around and under the car. Our driver wound down his window and told the duty sergeant, 'Thank you. I am carrying The Permanent Under-Secretary for Defence.'

The sergeant came to the rear window and looked in and snapped off a perfect salute. Then his face dropped, leaving his mouth and his eyes wide open in amazement. Sir Michael, who had turned off his reading light, was sitting in deep shadow on the far side of the seat and the only figure the sergeant could see was me, sitting there in my Franciscan habit. The poor man must have wondered what on earth one of his most exalted superiors was up to, dressed as a friar. Our car moved on and he probably never did get an answer.

The speaker at the Campion Dinner was usually a famous celebrity or high-ranking army officer, but in the following year I was invited to give the keynote speech to the cadets. It was the Sandhurst Chaplain, who arranges these dinners, who called me. He had been let down at the last minute by someone much more exalted and needed a stand-in. What I had not realized as a guest, was just how dangerous the earlier events could prove to be for an after-dinner speaker.

First there were drinks at the house of the Commandant, then Major General Arthur Denaro, on one's arrival. Then on to the Indian Room for a reception, where the drinks came fast and huge. And finally in to dinner, with copious amounts of wine being poured, followed by the passing around of many bottles of port. At which point, at around midnight, one was expected to stand up and make a coherent speech – albeit aimed at a rowdy audience of drunken cadets (plus various generals and the Commandant who were equally merry).

I found that when the time came, and I heard myself being introduced, unfortunately I was barely able to stand. I looked at the sea of grinning, flushed faces in front of me and any ideas I may have had about my speech were jettisoned on the spot.

'I wish to speak to you on the virtues of temperance,' I told them. They were well into the port by this time and started banging their glasses on the table. I cupped my hands to my mouth and shouted, 'As I said, I wish to speak to you on the virtues of temperance.' That got their attention.

'All I have to say is that aged eighteen everything went wrong when I became a Catholic. I never touched a drop before that. I was brought up in the Salvation Army where drink was considered evil, as we all know it is, and we must toast to that.' I raised my glass to much laughter, and everyone took a drink.

I continued, 'Then I became an even stricter temperance adherent when I became a Strict and Particular Baptist. But now, since I have become a Catholic I have been making up for lost time, for eighteen years of no drinking in fact.' The cadets were by now uncontrollable. Laughing and cheering my every sentence. I added a few more light-hearted comments then said something serious and affirming about their role and their offering their lives for their country, and sat down to a roar of applause.

The whole speech had taken a little under five minutes. I doubt that even the most talented stripper could have held those cadets' attention longer than that.

But that's just what another friend of mine, then editor of *The Daily Mirror*, Piers Morgan, tried to do a year later. I like Piers very much and he has always been helpful with charitable causes. But on that night, he did nobody any favours, including himself. As happened to me, it was after midnight when he came to make his speech, and even though I had tried to warn him about the reception he was going to receive, Piers stuck rigidly to the text he had prepared, and gave them a full half hour.

The suave and polished Piers Morgan you see today, he of the instant quip and twinkle-eyed confidence, was absent in the Piers who addressed the Sandhurst cadets that night. He ended deflated, flushed and perspiring. He simply had failed to judge his audience, who were all tipsy as usual, and made no allowances. He could have cut his speech by twenty minutes and no-one would have noticed – but he plodded doggedly on talking about the defence of the press and other media problems.

After a few minutes of this he had completely lost his audience. Some groups of cadets started their own conversations or were telling jokes, others just lay their heads on the table and went to sleep, or pretended to. There were even calls for him to sit down and some cadets started a slow hand-clap but to no avail. Piers persevered to the bitter end with his prepared speech.

I don't know how he felt afterwards but I felt embarrassed for him, poor man. I sincerely doubt that that particular night's performance will be featuring in any volume of his memoirs.

$\mathcal{N}$INETEEN

WRENCH OF LEAVING HOME – THE PIANO-PLAYING
BISHOP – GRAND NATIONAL OUSTS THE
ENTHRONEMENT – A SONG FOR THE POPE – THE
AMAZING, AMERICAN, DANCING MONSIGNOR
–SCANDAL FROM THE PAST BRINGS TROUBLE –
THE FALL GUY

After their experience with Hume, the monk, the Vatican was
uncertain about a successor and took a few months before
naming Cormac Murphy-O'Connor as the new Archbishop of
Westminster. Powerful factions within the Church had favoured
other candidates but none of them had attracted universal support,
and Cormac was seen, by many, as a good man and a safe pair of
hands to guide British Catholics into the new millennium.

The Catholic clergy had accepted him more readily than they
had Cardinal Hume, for like them he had been a diocesan priest.
But those who had campaigned for his rivals were inclined
neither to fully accept him nor give him the full support he
needed. I believe, like Hume, he was initially reluctant to accept
the post, and who can really blame him, if that was the case.

He had been a bishop for twenty-three years, living in a lovely
house in glorious countryside in a very quiet and secluded corner

of East Sussex. It was a sprawling building with large gardens and fantastic views across the South Downs, where he lived with his dogs, a private secretary and the several nuns who looked after him. I suspect, that being only human, it must have been a terrible wrench for him to leave his home in its idyllic setting and move into a brick monolith with no grass or trees in sight and lose the loyalty and support he had enjoyed from his faithful clergy and staff as Bishop of Arundel and Brighton.

Whereas Hume arrived with two suitcases, Cormac came with a full removal lorry – the removals company, I remember, was called 'Bishop's Move' – containing the furniture and belongings he had collected over a lifetime – including a grand piano. That made two grand pianos in Archbishop's House, and Cormac regularly played on them. He is an exceptional classical pianist and I would often hear him on one of the pianos when I was there, usually playing his favourites, Schubert and Chopin.

He was persuaded to play Schubert's *March Imperial* at one of the annual *Night Under The Stars* charity concerts raising funds for The Passage and he received a standing ovation.

As a priest he had played the guitar and sung in church. He has a fine voice and in his younger days gave a great rendition of some of the Beatles' hits. But when accompanying himself on the piano, he never sang pop songs – just Italian ballads. He had been Rector of the English College in Rome and had spent a total of fifteen years there all told. His Italian is fluent, and he knows many classical Italian pieces.

The only hitch with Cardinal Cormac's enthronement as the tenth Archbishop of Westminster came when we had to change the date of March 25th. The BBC told us they couldn't possibly film it on that day because of their coverage of the Grand National. There was no question of Aintree changing the date of the nation's favourite steeplechase – or of it not being televised – so we had to choose another date, three days earlier, the 22nd, for the enthronement.

Six weeks after that I told him that I was ready to leave, if he wished it. We were alone in his office when I suggested that it was, perhaps, time for me to go. I felt I had to give him that option in case he wanted to make a change. I had been there fifteen years – it is usual for a priest to be in a post four or five years and move on – and thought it might be time for me to find new challenges.

He was highly complimentary and very positive and said that he would like me to stay on in my responsibility for ecumenical affairs, given the extensive network of people whom I knew. I promised to check with him again in the new year to confirm this was still the case. The following January, his response was to come to my home for supper to tell me he wanted me to remain. I lived in the friary with another Franciscan, Brother Gerry, an American who had previously managed the Catholic Central Library when it was based in our friary building.

We understood that was the night Cormac was named a cardinal and we all enjoyed some champagne to celebrate my staying on, but it was probably just as much about Cormac getting his 'red hat'. The official announcement came in February.

The changes after Cormac moved in were quite dramatic. The way Hume had lived in Archbishop's House was as he had lived in the monastery, as a monk, occupying the smallest and least number of rooms he could manage with. He had a small bedroom and bathroom next to his den on the floor above the main floor where his office was, and that's where he preferred to relax. He claimed the formal rooms, below, were much too grand for him, and he rarely used them, except for official functions.

Cardinal Cormac turned it back into a home. His bedroom was the large, traditional one, next door to the office, which Hume always referred to as the Pope's room (because the Pope had showered and changed there during his visit to Britain in 1982). All previous cardinals had used it as their bedroom, except Hume.

Cormac had the reception rooms, Throne Room, drawing room, the library and private chapel, redecorated. They are each enormous spaces where Hume could never relax. He had few of them painted, and none, to my knowledge repaired in his twenty-three years there. In fact, he did so little that the house looked shabby and in need of repair when he died.

When he was in his office Hume almost always kept the door open so you could see him – and he could see out. It closed only rarely, for really private meetings. Cormac was a man who always kept the door closed, or partly closed, for privacy. Getting access to him was never easy and appointments had to be made in advance, for he believed in routine and order. In one way though he was far more casual than Hume, taking most of his meals in the nuns' dining room upstairs, or even in the kitchen. They would eat, as they lived together, like equals. His three Irish nuns, Sisters Clement, Barbara and Pius, would never put up with being treated as servants. They were wonderful Augustinian nuns who came with him from Burgess Hill, in Sussex, and he had known them for many years.

Cormac is very informal in some ways and would sometimes eat walking around, with a plate in one hand and a fork in the other. Wandering round and meeting everyone was more important to him than sitting at a table. The nuns would serve if he had a visitor stay to eat, an arrangement I had seen, but if there were no guests it was up to everybody to fend for themselves. I missed the banter which I had enjoyed so much with Cardinal Hume. Life in the Cathedral became a more serious and predictable affair under Cormac – though to give him his due, he was occasionally ready to join in the fun.

On Christmas Day and Easter Sunday when he lunched with everyone, he would always end up singing and would really relax.

The afternoon he flew back from Rome, after the election of Joseph Ratzinger as Pope Benedict XVI, he attended a lecture in the Cathedral given by Mary McAleese, the President of Ireland, and held a reception for her in the Throne Room afterwards. That evening we went to the Irish Embassy for another reception and dinner, and as usual with functions there, everybody became quite merry. Cardinal Cormac was in a good mood and being very entertaining, and during the reception told us all about his singing episode in Rome.

After the Pope had been shown to the people – *Habemus Papam* – a special dinner involving only the new Pope and his cardinals is held. Cormac said it was very cheerful and the champagne was flowing but nobody was singing. So he got up and said 'Holy father to congratulate you on this special occasion, perhaps we can all sing you a little song', and he started a song that they all knew – *Ad Multos Annos Viva*.

Unfortunately each nationality tends to have its own tune for this well known refrain – and none is like the English version. The one Cormac was singing was used by the English College. And he was the only Cardinal from England.

'It was very embarrassing,' he confessed to me. 'I had to make a quick decision. Do I sit down and shut up or do I carry on? So I decided to carry on. The Pope and all the cardinals stared at me as if I was stupid as I sang the whole thing. Then the Polish cardinals decided not to be outdone, and things started to liven up. There were several of them and they performed something in Polish. The Italians, of course, could muster a whole choir of cardinals. I was the only soloist.'

I responded and said, 'As you haven't become the 'White One' yet, you're unlikely to be changing your cassock in the future.'

'No, I won't,' he said.

'Does that mean that all that's left to you is death?' I asked innocently.

'I suppose so, yes,' he replied.

'Well have you decided which chapel you're going in? You have to be ready you know?'

He hinted that he might quite like St Patrick's Chapel in the Cathedral.

At a subsequent dinner, two extremely successful brothers from an Irish construction company, Joe and John Kennedy, were seated on either side of me, and I told them of the Cardinal's wish to be buried in St Patrick's Chapel. 'We'll bury him,' said Joe; 'We'll build the tomb,' echoed John.

I explained that the Chapel was not quite finished and we were looking for someone to complete it.

'We'll do it,' said Joe and John in unison.

The Cardinal was on the table next to us and I leaned backwards and said, 'I've found two people who want to bury you, and what's more they're going to finish St Patrick's Chapel before they put you in it.'

He was delighted and beamed his thanks at Joe and John, who toasted him enthusiastically. Sadly and much to the Kennedys' regret the Chapel is still unfinished, and there is quite definitely no sign of his tomb! Perhaps the Cardinal chose, for personal reasons, to put this project on a back burner.

This was something I am sure, in retrospect, he wished he had done when he elected to take over five hundred of his priests and bishops on a bonding trip to Butlin's Holiday Camp in Bognor, in his former diocese of Arundel and Brighton.

This trip was for all the clergy for the entire diocese of Westminster, including all the religious orders. At least five hundred of us. And you needed a very serious excuse – at least a death in the family – to get out of attending. The Cardinal had put out a three-line whip on this and we were all expected at Butlins on the evening of November 4th 2002. Special transport was laid on to take some of us, but most decided to travel by car. We were to stay there until noon on November 7th.

There were monks and friars and priests of every description – Benedictines, Franciscans, Jesuits, traditional clergy from the Brompton Oratory and Opus Dei, progressives and conservatives, a smattering of bishops – and a couple of cardinals for good measure, one of whom, the Primate of Belgium, Cardinal Godfried Daneels, a papal candidate, would give a keynote address.

We were each given a form in advance and asked to name a person with whom we wished to share a chalet, otherwise, we were told, we would be allocated a chalet with someone not of our choice – probably a complete stranger. People were running around for months trying to find a partner they could tolerate in their chalet. Someone who didn't snore, or smoke, or sniff or any of the other traits we couldn't get on with at close quarters. I proposed Father Richard Andrew, the then Sub-Administrator of the Cathedral, but had other names on a list in case he was booked. Fortunately he was agreeable and we were able to send our completed forms to the Cardinal in time.

The bishops were each given a separate chalet.

It was a most bizarre, almost surreal situation as the machines were all going when we arrived. Giant models, normally there to amuse the kids, which all seemed to move at the press of a button. Everything worked, even the rides – and the Redcoats were out in force to take care of us. On the walk from the big gala room, with its stage, to our dining room, all the giant figures would be moving and the slot machines and one-armed bandits would be alive, like in Las Vegas, going bing bing bing, bong bong bong, and there was music playing all the time.

In the middle of all these machines was a long bar and nearly everyone made a beeline for it. I doubt they had ever done business like it. It is always difficult to get clergy away from the bar. We couldn't leave the buildings because the weather was dreadful, freezing, arctic cold with a huge sea throwing up sheets of spray and constant, teeming rain.

It had been intended to leave the bar open all the time, but they found they had to close it to get the clergy into the meetings.

Some of the priests had arrived with bottles, relying on strong drink to get them through the three days, and there were many naughty chalets with noisy parties going on into the early hours. The holy chalets seemed to be in the extreme minority!

It was a very funny experience watching the priests and monks and friars standing at the slot machines with drinks in their hands, or sampling the children's rides. The whole point of this seaside excursion, explained Cardinal Murphy-O'Connor, at our first get-together, was to ask us whether we wanted renewal. How could one possibly vote against that? Everyone raised his hand and it was decided unanimously. Of course we wanted renewal. But it wasn't quite that simple.

What he was proposing, we only discovered after the vote, was the adoption of a new programme of renewal for the entire Diocese of Westminster which came from America. It was called 'Renew'. The Cardinal, it appeared, had already used this programme in his former diocese of Arundel and Brighton – though to the rest of us it was like a bolt from the blue. The English clergy, to say the least, do show a certain reluctance to change. Quietly cautious is perhaps a better way of putting it. New fangled ideas, especially those coming out of America, always set alarm bells ringing. And this 'program' was no exception. Had it come from Britain, or even Europe, it might have raised slightly less suspicion.

But coming from America, and from the amazing Monsignor who suddenly appeared on the stage, with massive flared drapes as a backdrop, it was all a bit too much...

The American was something of a cross between Sinatra and George Burns, with a bombastic personality and full of razzmatazz enthusiasm. Of course to the clergy it looked just like a performance. A well-rehearsed routine. And that's what it was. The Monsignor promised that all Church collections would increase through this programme: 'All your schools will be wonderful and your children will be gloriously educated,' he assured. He barely stopped short of promising perennial sunshine. He was aided by an American nun of the 'free range' variety, Sister Cheryl.

It was slick and fantastic and, of course, quite disturbing to the temperament of the English clergy. They went through stages of shock, through jaw-dropping disbelief, and finally into orbit. They had voted to be renewed. They hadn't voted 'Renew'. Some saw this as a *fait accompli*. The Cardinal had already invited these Americans to be there, and had them ready to appear on stage as soon as we had voted. Do you want renewal? Yes. Off went the Cardinal and on came the American performing troop. Some thought they had been victims of a sleight of hand – and they were not happy.

The Americans were not there giving their services free either. Some of the clergy raised the question of just how much this programme would cost. It appeared the Church paid substantially for the American troop to go around renewing dioceses. 'Renew', or 'At Your Word Lord' as it became known in the Diocese, was a programme intended to last three years. The clergy all respected the office of the archbishop, but that didn't mean them following him blindly into any venture.

To Cormac's credit he recognized this. Not surprising then that in the open session which followed the presentation, he came under a certain amount of pressure. Anyone had the right to speak, and to say what he wanted, and some of the speakers from the floor criticized his choice of programme and his introduction of it.

At the end of the day some seventy-five per cent of the diocesan parishes sincerely tried to use the renewal programme, and in so many ways it was successful. A lot of groups founded in those days still exist. Part of this 'renewal' was to encourage contact with other denominations and religions, and young people would go to churches for discos and social, as well as spiritual, events. Then they would host visitors from those churches in return. Some found it very rewarding.

On the eve of our departure from Bognor there was an extremely festive dinner, with celebrations that went on long into the early hours. The main toast on everyone's lips was that we would never again be called on to spend time together at another holiday camp. To which, I am sure, the Cardinal added a very sincere 'Amen'. I really can't see any other bishop trying to repeat this holiday-camp fiasco. He would be on a Hi-de-hi hiding to nothing.

In his last five years as Cardinal, Cormac blossomed, as his true worth became apparent to his detractors. But in the early years of his reign he was hounded by members of the Church, public and media. When this 'safe pair of hands' was enthroned in the year 2000, the Vatican was not aware of his role in a paedophile sex scandal involving a Catholic priest. There was, at the time, a worldwide outcry against paedophile priests in the Catholic Church and he, tragically, became the British focus of this international protest when it was reported in the media that while he was Bishop of Arundel and Brighton, Cormac had been warned that a priest in his charge, Father Michael Hill, who had sexually abused young children he met through his Church work, was a danger to young people.

The Bishop had revoked Hill's licence to work in a parish after the priest was implicated in indecent assaults on several young children in his care. Eighteen months later, Hill convinced Cormac he was a reformed character and the Bishop returned him to pastoral duties as chaplain at Gatwick Airport. There had been warnings from doctors and therapists that Hill was likely to re-offend but Cormac judged that as it was an industrial chaplaincy at Gatwick, it was extremely unlikely he would come into contact with single children. Police and social workers who were consulted, agreed that it was in order.

No-one could have anticipated that a young stowaway would seek the Priest's help and that Hill would offer a place for the boy to hide – and then, it was claimed by police, sexually assault him. A full police investigation was launched and all the previous complaints against Hill, spanning twenty years, came to light.

In court in 1997, Hill pleaded guilty to ten charges of indecent assault and gross indecency and was sentenced to five years in prison. He served only three years and was released the year Cormac became Archbishop of Westminster.

The BBC broke the story of Cormac's involvement, largely through BBC Radio 4's *Today* programme, and in an interview he said that he had been acting on the advice of professionals at the time, but added: 'Would I do that now in the light of the knowledge we have? I would say no I wouldn't.' The families of Hill's victims, and many others too, believed the Church should have done more, despite Cormac ordering compensation to be paid out to the abused children.

The whole question of child abuse and the clergy came to a crescendo that year and people were baying for blood. Cormac became a scapegoat, with the BBC and *The Times* demanding his resignation, and though he had done nothing improper himself, he was pilloried and maligned. The fact that he had asked the police and social services if it was safe for a paedophile to work in a restricted environment like Gatwick, and they had concurred, was not mentioned by most of the media. Some would have appointed Hill without reference to anyone, or banned him for life. Cardinal Cormac became the fall guy for the Catholic Church in Britain. He did not deserve such censure, unlike America's Boston Archdiocese which was guilty of covering up scores of incidents where priests had preyed on young children. It transpired the Archdiocese had secretly settled child molestation claims against at least seventy priests in the past decade. A US lawyer for some of the victims said, 'It's almost surreal that the supposed most moral institution in the world could act so immorally.'

Paedophile mania, which threatened to unseat Cormac, was always strong. At one time, protestors wanted to ban the music of Vivaldi in churches, because he was a priest and, apparently, a known child-abuser. The attack on Cardinal Murphy-O'Connor was always unfair and unjustified.

After overcoming the negative publicity which marred the first few years of his reign, Cardinal Cormac became a redoubtable moral force in the country and a champion for the preservation of human dignity in all its forms.

TWENTY

FUN NIGHTS AT STRINGFELLOWS – STRIPPER VICAR
MIX-UP – THE BOGUS PRIEST FIASCO –
CONSECRATED VIRGINS AT A BOOK LAUNCH –
SCANDALOUS CLERGY STORIES

I first met Peter Stringfellow at his famous night club on the
edge of Covent Garden when I went there with a friend, Noel
Botham, for dinner. Peter joined our table and seemed concerned
that I might be offended by the naked lap-dancers, who were just
starting their nightly gyrations in front of the eager, and free-
spending, male customers in the bar.

'Salome probably started the trend,' I told him. 'There is
nothing offensive about the human body: it is very well-
designed. Though I think some of our nuns are perhaps a lot
prettier.' He laughed when I assured him the Catholic Church
was not about to set up in opposition, and told me he was as
happy to contribute to our cause, as his customers were to his
girls. And he was true to his word. Apart from contributing to
my Heaven book – thoughts from celebrities and others on
what they thought heaven would be like – which raised money

for The Passage, Peter has been a generous supporter of many charities, and given of his time to help with several fund-raising events.

It is surprising, and not widely known, that one of his many fans is Baroness Thatcher. She attended a Tory-dominated Haven Trust charity event at Stringfellow's, and after brilliantly working the room – she shook the hand of virtually every one of the 340 guests present – she joined Peter on the dance floor downstairs before leaving. As she walked up the stairs, she turned and blew him a big kiss in front of everyone – never a person afraid to express her real feelings. What a Lady!

The strippers in Peter's club were the only ones I ever encountered in person, although on one, odd, occasion I was mistaken for a stripper myself. It happened in The Avenue, a large and very popular bar and restaurant in St James's Street, run by a charming lady manager. I had gone there in my working garb of black suit and dog collar to meet an army officer whose marriage I had solemnized and who was partying there with friends. I was running rather late as I dashed into the club, which was very crowded and noisy. As I stepped through the door a girl grabbed me by the arm and hissed, 'You're late. We've all been waiting for you.'

I thought it odd that everyone in the party had been told I was coming, but it was unimportant. I simply blurted an apology for being late and asked where she and the others were sitting, as I needed to go to the cloakroom before I could join them. 'We're over there in the corner,' she told me, and pointed above the heads of the crowd.

When I emerged from the lavatory, the girl was still waiting and took my arm and began leading me through the crush of people. Eventually we arrived in front of a group of young women. 'Here he is,' said my guide.

'You're not the right group,' I said.

'Yes, we are,' she insisted. 'I booked you and you're performing for us. I was the one who hired you.'

'Nobody hired me,' I told her. 'I'm not available by the hour.'

'Yes we did,' she said. 'You're our stripper-gram vicar.'

I told them I was terribly flattered, but I was afraid I would not be performing for them that night, or any other night for that matter. 'I've got to tell you that you'd be very disappointed if I did,' I apologized.

It transpired they were a hen party and I was supposed to entertain the bride-to-be.

'I'm afraid you'll have to go out on to the street and grab another vicar,' I said, and left them giggling in embarrassment at mistaking the real thing for the showman. Eventually I did find my right party and all ended well. And I kept my clothes on.

There was not such a happy ending on another embarrassing occasion when a woman in a club accused me of being an imposter and I was thrown out. It all took place in the Groucho Club in Soho's Dean Street, the famous watering hole frequented by actors and other celebrities. I had been to a book launch nearby and had promised to meet up with friends at the bar in Grouchos. I couldn't spot them and headed across to the long bar to buy a drink and wait for their arrival. As I approached, a woman, who was rather the worse for drink, accosted me and pointing a shaking finger at my dog collar, told me: 'You're not a priest! You're an actor pretending to be a priest.'

Had I been in my friar's habit, I might have understood it, but I was wearing a dark suit and dog collar and looked perfectly normal.

'I can assure you that I am a priest,' I told her. 'Well prove it,' she retorted. 'If you're a priest tell me the ten commandments.' I managed to get nine out of ten, which I thought wasn't too bad after the few drinks I had consumed at the book launch earlier.

'Rubbish,' howled the woman. 'Now name me the seven deadly sins.'

I should have walked away at that point, but I didn't. I managed to name six of the deadly sins, and again didn't think I had done badly.

The woman started to shout. 'I told you that you weren't a real priest and I was right. You can't even remember all ten commandments or the seven deadly sins.' Then she started to push me. 'I'm going to expose you. You fraud! He's not a priest,' she screamed. 'He can't name the ten deadly sins!'

I was about to retort 'commandments' but it was the moment the barman took us for a couple of crazies and called security. We were both thrown out.

Outrageous humour has always appealed to me, and in clerical terms I have encountered no prankster more outrageous than the Reverend David Johnson, who, with the Reverend Toby Forward, in 1994 wrote *The Spiritual Quest of Francis Wagstaffe*.

They wrote to over fifty established Church of England bishops, asking a variety of strange questions. In the earlier of the letters, Francis posed as a purveyor of Cumberland sausages and former prep school proprietor who was seeking guidance on the Christian faith, and in the later letters he poses as His Grace the Most Reverend the Archbishop of the Old Northern Catholick Church of the East Riding Mar Francis II Metropolitan and Primate, Knight Grand Commander of the Order of Saint John of Beverly (1st Class).

One such letter, written to the then Bishop of Bristol, Barry Rogerson, went thus: 'My nephew, Colin, intends offering himself as a candidate for ordination. He has reformed himself from being a somewhat wayward youth... When he was much younger he got involved in a rather 'theatrical' set, as a result of which he ended up with a tattoo on the back of his left wrist of an anchored heart surmounted with the word "Kevin". This is not immediately obvious but it is there beneath his cuff for anyone to see who is in the know. Colin's vicar in Brighton laughs this off simply as *folie de jeunesse* and says nobody these days would be bothered... Perhaps you may think me old fashioned, but I think it will count against him at his selection board, and he ought to have it removed before he presents himself.'

The Bishop wrote back almost by return: '...I am sure the selectors are, as the scripture says, looking at the heart rather than the outward appearance of a candidate... I have no idea how many people have been recommended for training who have a tattoo of the variety you describe, but do I know of at least one... so I hope this will put your mind at rest.'

David Johnson, sometime President of the Oxford Union, also produced *Not the Church Times*, a *Private Eye*-style magazine which printed outrageous and scandalous stories about the clergy. It was hilariously funny, utterly indiscreet and pilloried by the Church hierarchy. For this 'crime' he was ejected from the staff of the Archbishop of Canterbury and sent to look after several isolated rural parishes in the wilds of Leicestershire. The banishment of this extremely intelligent and perceptive priest has been, I believe, a great loss to the Church of England. I concur wholeheartedly with many of his colleagues, who still refer to him as 'the finest bishop the Church of England never had'.

As for Toby Forward, I understand he was once hailed by Virago Press as the precursor to Zadie Smith or Monica Ali, having written a slim volume of passionate love stories under the assumed name of Rahila Kahn. Virago Press had been conceived in the early 1970s 'as the first mass-market published for fifty-two per cent of the population – women' and they continue only to publish books penned by women. Rahila's – or Toby's – book, which supposedly lifted the lid on Asian women's experiences in London, was trumpeted as a sensation. Pleading Rahila's parents' disapproval, the 'authoress' shunned publicity and book launches – including refusing for any photograph of her to appear on the cover; she was after all a shy twenty-something living on a housing estate somewhere in London. When Virago Press finally discovered the true identity of the literary genius they were not at all amused and the to-be best-selling first novel *Down the Road Worlds Away* was pulp.

I went to the book launch of *The Spiritual Quest of Francis Wagstaffe* at the Atheneum Club in Pall Mall. It was a spectacular affair with a host of secular and clerical personalities present. The waitresses, looking very unappealing and frumpish, were dressed as consecrated virgins and wore little veils. I thought it most unlikely that anyone in his right mind would want to deconsecrate them! Norman St John Stevens, the man who invented 'the blessed Margaret' tag for Mrs Thatcher was there, talking with then Tory MP, Neil Hamilton and his wife Christine. I joined them and learned that Neil was very interested in religion and was a High Anglican with extreme Catholic tendencies. Despite all the adverse reports, I found the Hamiltons to be a fun couple then, and during a friendship that has spanned fifteen years, I have always found them to be both entertaining and charming.

TWENTY-ONE

A WAKE FOR THE TORIES – CYNTHIA PAYNE AND
HER HOUSE OF SIN – THE HUMAN FACE OF BRITISH
MONARCHY – IN HENRY VIII'S DUNGEONS – MAGIC
CARPET RIDE – JEFFREY ARCHER AND FORGIVENESS
– MASTER OF THE BREAD ROLLS – FREEING THE
SPIRITS IN SOHO – A 'MAP-MAN' IN L.A.

The end of the Conservative party's eighteen year domination of British politics, in 1997, prompted several bizarre wakes around London, and almost certainly in other parts of the country too, as Tories drowned their sorrows after their kamikaze-like plunge into near oblivion.

The first such wake to which I had been invited was hosted by *The Daily Telegraph* at Christopher's in the Strand. The 'party' did not last long as the Conservative politicians there became increasingly more depressed and found it beyond them to maintain any kind of party spirit. I left a couple of them crying real tears into their drinks and went on to what had always promised to be the best wake in town.

Robert Smith, a good friend of twenty years, acted as agent for those hereditary peers who wanted to sell off their Lords of the Manor titles, some of whom had fallen on hard times.

Anticipating the debacle to come, Robert had sent out black-edged invitations, summoning people to a funeral party. An ancient black hearse was parked outside his impressive Georgian Kennington house and the front door was draped in black bunting. Inside, there were further black drapes everywhere and he had placed little television sets all around the house, and even in the garden, so the attending, by now mournful, Conservatives could watch the results come in and suffer together.

There were a number of Tory MPs and peers I recognized who were, like their party, already on the way to temporary oblivion, and determined to celebrate to the hilt as the Party ship went down. One very sober early guest was a favourite MP friend of mine, Nirj Deva, who was destined to lose his seat for Brentford and Isleworth later that night – though he bounced back as a Conservative MEP two years later. Nirj is Sri Lankan-born and acts every inch the Colonial Governor: extremely British and very conservative. One nickname fellow MPs have for him is 'The Viceroy', but usually he is fondly referred to as 'His Excellency', because he is so grandly imperial in style. His marriage (in 1989) to Indra, his lovely French-speaking wife from Mauritius (which I performed) was a splendid event.

Coming face to face with a friend like Nirj at social gatherings was not at all unusual, but more often than not the people I came into contact with while working were either total strangers or people with whom I had only slight acquaintance. As a chaplain to Westminster Hospital in my early days at the Cathedral, I would often encounter MPs and peers from the Palace of Westminster, which was then close by (the hospital has since been moved to Fulham). When visiting a Catholic patient, I would always try to talk to the people in the beds on either side, regardless of their religion.

I found most people welcomed a friendly word and a bit of compassion when they were in hospital. I rarely knew their names but when I did learn someone's identity I was occasionally quite surprised. I was chatting to one woman patient I just knew as Audrey when her husband came in. It was James 'Sunny Jim' Callaghan, the former Labour Prime Minister and still then an MP. He was surprised a Catholic priest had bothered to come over and say 'Hello' as he and his wife were confirmed Baptists.

One of the most interesting chance meetings I had was with Cynthia Payne, whose 'house of sin' in suburban Streatham catered for middle aged and elderly judges, lawyers, MPs and peers, who would exchange their 'luncheon vouchers' for food, drink, a nice chat and a romp in a bedroom with their favourite among Cynthia's 'beautiful helpers'. Very close to her house of ill repute was a convent, run by nuns, where I gave a retreat in 1987.

Cynthia was a regular visitor to the many religious establishments in the area, and a supporter of the nuns. She told me she was great chums with some of the local clergy, of various callings, though I thought it best not to probe too deeply into their precise relationship.

The famous court case, which kept the whole nation entertained for several weeks with tales of the burlesque antics and bawdy goings on, was something else, although in the end, Cynthia won a resounding victory and was found innocent of all

255

nine charges of controlling prostitutes; she became something of a celebrity because of that case and the subsequent film about her life, *Personal Services*, starring Julie Walters. She was always willing to open local bazaars and fund-raising galas if they were for a good cause, and helped publicize all the local church charity events – usually giving generously herself.

One lady, of a <u>very</u> different ilk, and of whom I am particularly fond, is The Duchess of Kent, the former Katherine Worsley, who I first met in 1985, shortly after my arrival at the Cathedral. She visited our friary in London three years later to unveil a plaque to her friend, the former Bishop of Leeds, William Gordon Wheeler, who had been instrumental in my Order of Friars coming to London in July 1959.

She had formed a close friendship with Cardinal Hume almost from the moment he was appointed in 1976, though of course, being Yorkshire-born she had been acquainted with him when he was still Abbot of Ampleforth. Kate, a sweet and gentle lady, was received into the Catholic Church in January 1994 by Cardinal Hume, who personally arranged her very special service, which took place in his private chapel in Archbishop's House. Her husband, The Duke of Kent, and all their children were there.

Another well known personality who chose to convert to Catholicism that same year of 1994 was MP and former cabinet minister, John Gummer. John's father had, like me, started out as a Baptist, subsequently becoming an Anglican and eventually a canon at Rochester Cathedral; John, himself a very High Church Anglican, had once considered becoming a monk. His conversion, unlike that of Ann Widdecombe, was a very private affair and he issued a statement only after the service, which was held in the Church of the Sacred Heart in Horseferry Road.

His fifteen-year-old son, Benedict, also chose to be received into the Church on the same day, and his wife Penny, the former Private Secretary to Edward Heath, and three other children, Felix, Leonora and Cordelia (who have since been received into the Church), were all there to support them. John, who had been one of eighteen strong Guardians of the beautiful Anglican Shrine to Mary, Mother of God, at Walsingham, was allowed to continue in that role, even though he had become a Catholic.

One of the regular features of parish life at Westminster Cathedral was the annual outing of the Friends, usually accompanied on their visitations to notable places by one of the Cathedral chaplains. In 1998, I was the chaplain who was lucky enough to accompany them on a visit to Windsor Castle, something I had been able to arrange with my friend, Canon John White, who was then Sub-Dean of St George's Chapel in the Castle.

However, the itinerary organized for the group raised a few eyebrows – we were due to arrive at Henry VIII Gate – not to many Catholic sensibilities a happy place – and from there we would go directly to the dungeon for coffee at 9.30am. Mass was due to follow at 10.00am, again in the dungeon, and then our two talks would also be held in the dungeon. After this, there was to be a tour of the castle and I thought there might be the possibility of some light relief and we would have tea elsewhere, but no, we were due back in the dungeon, before our departure, once again leaving the castle again by Henry VIII Gate. I told the secretary to look on our guest list in case we had inadvertently put down Guy Fawkes's name. As it happened our hosts were extremely kind to us but I still noticed, as our coach left Windsor, that some of our party seemed relieved to be leaving without a trip to the torture chamber.

One piece of 'torture' endured by an Anglican I knew, was the fuss which ensued on what turned out to be the non-appointment of Dr Geoffrey John, the gay, Elton John lookalike clergyman as Anglican Bishop of Reading. His abortive appointment as bishop had prompted a huge African / American Anglican backlash against his appointment and caused bitter division, because of matters relating to homosexuality. The Archbishop of Canterbury, Rowan Williams, forced Dr John to stand down as Reading's intended bishop, though he was subsequently appointed as Dean of St Alban's Abbey.

In July 2004, the Cardinal asked me to represent him at the installation of the new Dean and I accompanied our own Bishop Jim, James O'Brien. The massive clerical turn out for John's inauguration as Dean showed the great support he still retained. Hundreds of clergy – Anglicans, Catholics and Methodists among them – turned out to express their support. The procession at the start was so packed with clergy wanting to show solidarity that the service took two hours in all.

The Bishop of St Alban's, Christopher Herbert, told the congregation of more than 2,000, he had been aware, when considering Geoffrey John's appointment, that reactions to it might be mixed. 'There are very, very many who are absolutely thrilled; and there are some of my fellow Christians who have been – and remain – deeply upset, angry and dismayed. What we have to do is listen deeply and patiently to each other so that understanding on all sides may grow,' he told them. He talked of John's pain and persecution and the hate mail he had received, and at the end of his sermon he received a standing ovation.

Police had expected a major demonstration outside the Abbey by opponents to a self-confessed gay priest (with a fellow priest as his partner) becoming Dean of St Albans. Security was on red alert. In the event a lone protestor turned up, the Reverend David Grade, a 'bishop' of the African Church in Liverpool, carrying a placard featuring Sodom and Gomorrah and shouting about God blowing up the Abbey. Ironically, of course, he had rather missed the point of the story of Sodom and Gomorrah which was much more to do with lack of hospitality and prayer.

The procession to conclude Geoffrey John's inauguration service promised to be just as long and time-consuming as at the start and after almost two hours, I couldn't wait until it had ended and still hope to make my train to London on time. I had to get away before the service finished as I was due at a dinner at the Dorchester Hotel in London's Park Lane that night to take part in a discussion which would feature the King of Jordan speaking on inter-faith issues, with the Duke of York there to represent the Queen. Benazir Bhutto, a most amazing lady, was also present, though sadly she later fell victim in her home country to a terrorist's bullet.

I managed to slip out in advance of the bishops and priests recessing to the vestry, still wearing my friar's habit, but despite the lack of protest, the police had locked the Abbey gates after everyone was inside, under a pre-arranged security plan and nobody was seemingly available with keys. My only option seemed to be to climb over the high, iron fence which encircled the Abbey.

I was perched halfway over, straddling the top rail, clutching my habit between my legs, when a policeman rushed over and demanded to know what I was up to. How the late Cardinal Hume would have laughed!

In hindsight, I guess it wasn't clear whether I was trying to get in or get out, making me a potentially dangerous protestor.

'I'm a one man escape committee,' I told him. 'The wages of sin are death,' said the lone protestor, shaking his placard, happy, after two hours, to have found someone apart from the police to protest to. I jumped down from the fence and told the constable: 'Have a nice day, officer, but I must run. I'm keeping a monarch and a prince waiting.' He must have thought I was as batty as the bearer of the placard, for he just removed his cap and scratched his head as I legged it, habit flapping, for the station.

At the opening of The Passage House, the Night Centre for The Passage, in January 2000, two of the charity's most enthusiastic supporters, the Duchess of Kent and Rory Bremner, were there to cut the ribbon and cheer on the proceedings.

Rory, who had become very anti Labour, had written a mocking Lord's Prayer, which he did in Tony Blair's voice, as the PM's special prayer to his God. It began: 'Our Father, who art New Labour, give us this day our daily electorate.... And free us from all Tories,' and was hilarious.

I had heard him recite it once before and had told the Duchess about it. She asked if he would do it for her. She, and all those within earshot, howled with laughter.

Tony, I'm sure, would also have found it funny. But Cherie might not have been amused.

As a small boy I thrilled to the story of Sinbad the Sailor in the *One Thousand and One Arabian Nights*, a collection of miraculous tales of exciting travel and mythical places – but never dreamed I might experience similar exotic adventures. Yet thanks to the generosity of some of my friends who have their own, distinctive, magic carpets, that is just what happened.

None of them, however, was more spectacular than that in 2003, when I was one of fifty guests invited to take an Arabian-nights style trip on one of the planes of Nadhmi Auchi, the billionaire Iraqi industrialist, who narrowly escaped from Saddam Hussein, after his brother had already been brutally murdered on the dictator's direct orders. Nadhmi owned General Mediterranean Holdings, which has numerous luxury hotels around the world.

We took off in the large jet from Stansted, bound for Beirut, where his latest, magnificent, five-star hotel was to open. There was an interesting mix of politicos, various City bigwigs, and, for good measure, at least one well-known spy.

During our journey we were served a spectacular meal and wines and entertained by beautiful hostesses in what seemed like a giant drawing room. The adventure continued in similar style – with a selection of gorgeous belly dancers weaving their magic.

My everlasting memory of that night will be when former Chancellor, Norman Lamont, and surprisingly, MP Alan

Duncan, impulsively leapt to the floor and danced well into the night with these voluptuous ladies!! So impressed by their performance was David Steel that he too took to the floor to partner one of the enticing dancers

A fascinating glimpse of the Arab world, albeit a distorted and luxurious one.

A year later I was again Mr and Mrs Auchi's guest, this time in his amazing Gulf Stream magic carpet, flying from Biggin Hill to a star-studded 50th birthday party in Sardinia. It was the opening leg of a scarcely believable few days.

I enjoyed another lavish lunch in the sky, sitting next to my friend Anthony Bailey, who among other things was public relations consultant to ex-King Simeon of Bulgaria, then his country's Prime Minister. It was the king's friend, Spas Roussev, whose birthday we were celebrating.

I was still eating my dessert when we landed in Sardinia where we were quickly whisked away to one of the world's most exclusive hotels, the Hotel Cala di Volpe, occupying much of the Bay of Foxes on the glimmering Costa Smerelda.

Rooms cost £1500 a night plus, per person, but were packed with the rich and famous, with others, unsuccessfully I might add, despite the large sheaves of cash being waved about, trying to haggle themselves a lodging for one extra night.

The place was awash with the sort of faces you would normally expect to see on a Hollywood screen or the most glitzy magazines.

Prince and Princess Michael of Kent were at the bar and seemed a little astonished to see a priest checking in. Though not as astonished as some of the other guests, namely the naked ladies who were sunbathing around the swimming pool. When they spotted my dog collar they leapt from their sun-loungers, arms windmilling to cover their exposed bits, and dived or jumped into the pool. Whether to save me or themselves embarrassment, I'm not sure. It appeared that visiting priests were an extreme rarity. Anthony Bailey suggested I wear civvies for the rest of my stay to allow the ladies to sunbathe un-flustered.

One man who welcomed my company was ex-King Victor Emmanuel of Italy who couldn't have been kinder. I spent a long time talking with him and his beautiful Swiss wife. I showed him the letters contained in a copy of my Heaven book, which he coveted so much that, sadly, I had no option but to give it to him – even though it had been intended as my gift to the Bulgarian birthday boy, who received an identical copy later.

Considering the quality of the guests I was astonished that the rooms were so plain and small. Anthony Bailey's room was so tiny his wardrobe was outside on the verandah. People were coming and going all the time by helicopter and there was a constant toing and froing from the marina of butlers and maids who were sleeping on their master's or mistress's yachts.

For the buffet lunch the next day many of the guests – including the royals – were in shorts. You had to look twice at some of the women to see if they were wearing costumes at all and – with my dog collar safely in a drawer in my room – I noticed several were not.

It was a bit like Bognor Regis – but filled with incredible people. And I agree with the late King George V on the subject of Bognor. In my experience it's a place where most residents claim to live in Chichester rather than admit to being Bognorians

The Auchis decided to leave a day early for our next destination, which was Belgrade, where Mr Auchi, Anthony Bailey and others were to be made Papal Knights, and I was to receive the Vatican *Cross Pro Ecclesia et Pontifice*, for my ecumenical work. I stayed the night with the Auchis in a Belgrade hotel.

There were several others there to receive Papal Knighthoods: Professor Nasser David Khalili, who is the foremost writer on, and collector of, Islamic art in the world, and Mahmoud Khayami, an Iranian born industrialist. Both were, as the Auchis, outstanding philanthropists.

Seven people were recognized for their contributions to ecumenical and inter-religious concerns and their assistance to the needs of people in Serbia and Kosovo. The Papal Nuncio, Archbishop Eugenio Sbarbaro, presented the scrolls and insignia on behalf of Pope John Paul II. It was fascinating that Muslims, Christians and Jews were honoured at the same time and that only three were Christians.

After we had received our awards – given in the Vatican Embassy in Belgrade - David Khalili invited myself and Anthony Bailey to fly with him to the South of France and stay at his house in St Raphael, near Nice. This time it was courtesy of the Professor's magic carpet. One could so easily get used to it – but no fear of that, for I was about to be brought abruptly down to earth and reality – by experiencing the joys, and necessary penance, of Easyjet!

But there was a happy ending.

Cardinal Cormac gave a special dinner in my honour to celebrate my having received the papal award. Though, to be honest, I am embarrassed about displaying it... In fact, I have only worn it on one occasion since that night, and for just five minutes... before taking it off to stop clerical and other jealous eyes seeing it!

One person I have found to be frequently misunderstood is the author Jeffrey Archer, Lord Archer of Sandwell. I have known him for twenty-five years and have always enjoyed his company. He is a charming, witty and amusing companion, a generous host and one of the best after-dinner speakers I have ever encountered... and I have sat through a few in my time.

It has become fashionable almost, among journalists and television presenters and pundits, to revile him as a person, and ridicule his writing skills at every opportunity. This shameful persecution comes from people who, for the most part, have never met him. Millions of copies of his novels have been sold worldwide, which I believe speaks adequately for his writing skills.

As for his crime of perjury, he has served his time in prison and wiped the slate clean. It cost him his political career and the excellent chance of becoming Mayor of London. Put simply, he lied to his wife and, having done so, he found he had to lie to everyone else thereafter. Any decent Christian knows that forgiveness is one of God's greatest gifts to us. Perhaps it is time for those who bear him so much ill-will to use this gift of God and forgive Jeffrey his sin.

It was forgiveness which prompted him to ask for my help, three years ago, in writing his then latest book, *The Gospel*

According to Judas. Judas is one of the most despised men in history and it is akin to using a swear word to call someone 'a Judas'. But one should remember also that St Peter denied Christ three times after his arrest. And St Paul, the public executioner, put to death the first martyr, St Stephen, before he became a Christian. Jeffrey wanted to 'redeem' Judas and wrote the Gospel through the eyes of Judas's son, Benjamin Iscariot, who had been mocked all his life for being the son of a traitor. It was, I think, a fantastic exposition about forgiveness.

Jeffrey wanted his book to reflect the best of biblical exegesis (study and understanding) and had found difficulty reaching the right people to help his research. Fortunately, I was able to introduce him to someone considered to be one of the world's finest biblical scholars, Cardinal Carlo Maria Martini, the former Archbishop of Milan, a good friend of the late Cardinal Hume and high on the list of possible future popes until the election of Pope Benedict XVI.

Cardinal Martini thought the project was an inspiring and good initiative and received us for an hour-and-a-half in Rome. He also recommended the man he believed would be the best biblical scholar to assist Jeffrey in his research – one of Martini's former students, named Professor Father Francis Moloney, an Australian from a teaching Order, the Salesians, who became Jeffrey's full-time collaborator and a dear friend. He was also a fellow cricket fanatic.

In 2006, we arranged for the book to be launched at the Pontifical Biblicum in Rome which the Rector kindly hosted. Jeffrey and Francis Maloney gave a lecture to students and various leading Catholics in the academic world.

It is always so easy to make mistakes or false assumptions – especially in relation to sin – but on one particular occasion in 2004, everyone in Harrods jumped to the wrong conclusion...

I had taken the Papal Ambassador (Nuncio), Archbishop Eugenio Sbarbaro, the Nuncio to Serbia, to the store to have tea with Mohamed Al Fayed. I had known the Nuncio for nearly thirty years, since he was a priest at the Vatican Embassy in Washington and I was a friar student at university there. He was in his full regalia, the cassock with the scarlet buttons, sash, cap and the ring. He had served in countries under five dictators, and got on with Mohamed like a house on fire. After tea, the Harrods' Chairman insisted he get the 'full treatment' and be piped around the store by his personal piper.

What I had not known was that it was 'Italian week' at Harrods and all the floors were dressed in an Italian theme, with the country's colours and flag everywhere. The Nuncio was Italian and when we reached the food hall, where many Italians were working, they all went crazy, kneeling down and kissing his ring and offering him little cheeses and titbits to eat. We made a triumphal tour of the store, ending up with an Italian-themed dinner in the restaurant with Mohamed. The Papal Nuncio told him he had never enjoyed himself quite so much. I didn't tell him that everyone believed he had been brought over by Mohamed especially to celebrate Italian week at Harrods – though come to think of it, the wily Chairman had invited us to visit him there when he discovered the Nuncio was in town.

I have always been blessed with a sense of humour, though on occasions it has threatened to get me into trouble, as I often speak before I have properly thought things through. It was touch and go the first time I encountered Lord Woolf, then the Master of the Rolls, the third most senior judge in England and Wales (who, in 2000, went on to become Lord Chief Justice, the second most senior judge in the UK). He is a tireless worker for Christian-Jewish understanding and we were both guests at a Jewish-Christian dinner at the Royal Society of Medicine in Wimpole Street, set up by my friend, Sir Sigmund Sternberg, the Hungarian-born Jew and British philanthropist. Ten of us had been invited to have a discussion about the similarities of Jewish and Christian principles.

A waitress with a tray of rolls was about to start serving them to the ladies present when I stopped her. 'You can't start with them,' I told her. 'It's not appropriate. You have to start with him,' and I pointed a finger across the table at Lord Woolf.

'But we always serve the ladies first,' retorted the waitress.

'No,' I repeated, 'you must start with him. He is the Master of the Rolls and responsible for all the rolls in Britain.' The waitress dutifully served the first roll to Lord Woolf, as the other guests began laughing. Woolf looked hard at me and for a moment I thought I had played the clown with the wrong man, especially as I had never met him before. Then his face creased and he began to laugh heartily.

On the morning of September 11th 2001, I arrived in Soho at the famous Bohemian bar and restaurant the French House, for over a century a meeting place for actors, writers, artists and poets, where its owner, the lovely Lesley Lewis, and her staff, had been troubled by ghosts in the cellars which stretch out under the road.

I carried with me my Bible and a bottle of Holy Water, with which – and with the aid of prayers – I proposed to seek to banish the non-drinkable spirits from the building.

But I was first to have lunch with friends Noel Botham and Derek Ive, the brilliant British press photographer from Madrid. We had planned to eat in the Union Club, in Greek Street, a Private Members' Club with a superb restaurant. We had only just received our starters when Derek Ive's mobile phone rang. It was a colleague in Malaga, Spain, telling him to get to a television set, because a plane had just flown into one of the twin towers of the World Trade Center in New York.

We called out the news to everyone in the restaurant and suddenly there was a hush. Then Derek received news that a second plane had struck the second tower. We passed the news on to the restaurant staff just as other mobiles began to ring and the club owners turned on a television in the bar and we could see the whole, hellish nightmare unfolding three-and-a-half thousand miles away. None in the restaurant that day felt like finishing the plates before them.

When we returned to the French House a few minutes later, through suddenly deserted streets, the customers and staff there were exhibiting the same kind of shock we had just left behind in the Union, and which I'm certain was being experienced by tens of millions of people at that moment around the world. Lesley suggested I say a prayer, and some of the customers knelt as I said prayers for the dying in New York, Washington and elsewhere. Several people were either openly crying or very near to tears. It was a very subdued group of us who descended to the cellar to complete the job I had originally gone there to do.

As I ordered these lost and tortured souls to leave the premises I could not help but think of the thousands of new souls, violently liberated from their bodies by the terrorist attacks in America, who were now seeking a safe and lasting haven. Altogether a most horrific and deeply disturbing day.

Having studied for several years at an American University in Washington, I try to take some of my holidays over there to keep in touch with old friends from my student days. One such visit, to meet up with a former friar classmate, Father Dan Callahan, was to Los Angeles in 1992. Dan was the Parish Priest of our Church there, St Odilia's – St Odilia was a Frenchwoman who had been born blind, though had her sight restored when she was anointed with the Oil of Chrism at her Baptism.

My visit to Dan followed in the wake of the acquittal of four Los Angeles police officers of assault in the brutal, videotaped beating of a black motorist, Rodney King, which subsequently led to serious riots erupting, in various predominantly black or Hispanic sections, in the city of the angels. I was staying in a very modest friary in South Central LA where some of the worst rioting was experienced. People were subsequently amazed that I had gone there for a holiday, though had I possessed the gift of foresight, I told them, I would not have been there at that time...

In the friary, one had to go through the kitchen, from the bedrooms, to get to the bathroom and lavatory, and that's just what I did at 3am one morning, except that the kitchen door slammed locked behind me and shut me off from my room. I was left on the wrong side of the door and stark naked; it was a warm May night and I was sleeping in the buff – not a problem as only men stayed in the friary.

After using the bathroom and realising my predicament, I found an office where there were bunches of keys – but none of them seemed to fit the right door which would release me back to my bed. After some minutes of disconcertion, I also discovered a pile of maps and a roll of Sellotape and saw a novel way of covering my naked body.

I decided to wrap myself in the maps and Sellotape them together; not exactly a Savile Row effort, but at least they covered the essentials. I had regained my modesty, if not a bed. One of the doors I tried eventually led me out on to the front lot, where there was a bench on the front porch. This time I did not care when the door clicked shut behind me – they must have been on spring-loaded closers – for I had found somewhere to lay my head for the rest of the night.

Not that I got much sleep. People were still rioting in nearby streets and the wail of police sirens, circling police helicopters and intermittent gun fire kept me awake all night long. The church was open and people were praying for peace, but how could I go in dressed in maps? It was only later that I thought I could perhaps have made my way to the sacristy to seek an alb – a full-length garment worn under priestly vestments – but I think the devout local residents may have misconstrued my motives should I have attempted such a thing.

So I lay or sat on the bench until the sun came up and half-heartedly broke through the LA morning pollution. Then I was spotted by a small squad of patrolling riot police, dressed like space troopers, who wandered over. 'Well what have we got here?' said one.

'That's what you call Map Man,' drawled another. 'A superhero, like Batman, who's afraid of not being able to find his way anywhere, let alone home.' They all began to laugh and I stood there, clutching my map costume around me, and feeling very foolish indeed. What had seemed to be a brilliant idea at 3am didn't look quite so hot now, facing a group of spectators which was swelling in number, as passers-by paused to see what was going on. All I could think was that I provided at least a little light relief after a stressful night.

I have never been so pleased to see anyone as the visiting Capuchin Friar, who arrived and opened the front door. He was rather at a loss for words too. Nonetheless, I was able to shuffle indoors with a modicum of dignity while the applause, whistles and catcalls from the LA cops and other spectators resounded outside. In the end, no harm was done, except to my pride – which as we know always comes before a fall – and I was able to have a good laugh about it safely back in London.

$\mathscr{E}$PILOGUE

This then is the end of my story to date. I still marvel, looking back at the last twenty-five years, that a child who was raised in a Manchester slum could end up as a priest chatting casually to the Queen and her children, and cracking jokes with the Prime Minister in his home. When Cardinal Hume picked me out as his ecumenical advisor in 1988 and pointed me in the direction of the Palace of Westminster, neither he nor I could have foreseen the eventful associations it would lead to. I am forever grateful to him, and to his successor, Cardinal Cormac Murphy-O'Connor, who led the singing, in July 2008, of 'For he's a jolly good fellow' at my farewell party in the Cathedral Hall, for their unstinting support over twenty years, until I relinquished my position at the Cathedral to move on to other things, including, I hope, a very well earned sabbatical and a new ministry.

I treasure very deeply all the memories brought to life in this book for richer or poorer. I have tried to recount as best I can scenes that are life-giving and hopeful. And though I consider myself firmly in the Sinner category, I hope to escape, at least occasionally, into a more Saintly place, and in any event, throw myself on the mercy of Our Creator, God.

$\mathcal{A}$UTHOR'S NOTE

As the late Margaret, Duchess of Argyll observed in the opening words of her autobiography *Forget Not* published in 1975, 'some moments of your life, you never forget no matter how long you live'. I still have the copy of the book which the dear Duchess dedicated to me at Christmas 1987. It was a first edition, though was perhaps not a copy which the Duchess should have been giving away as it contained a large stamp of the North East Scotland Library Service on the front page. This has continued to cause me pangs of conscience as to whether I should return the book, but I fear the fine after nearly thirty-five years of its first acquisition may be more than a humble friar could afford!

I offer the past twenty-five years as a simple memory in this book – I hope and pray happy memories for the most part, and for the sour memories, apologies if self-indulgent. I have tried to be as open as possible and as life-giving as I can – trying to use humour as a healing tool and at times to show our basic saintliness. For the sinners, which is very much my category, eternal hope – and a way out – thank God for change!

In publishing this book on the Feast of St Bonaventure, a thirteenth-century Italian Franciscan once selected to be Archbishop of York but never consecrated, I offer humble prayer. However, I trust my fate may be more benevolent than Bonaventure's: he died under suspicious circumstances – possibly poisoned – and I am sure there are some who would plot such mysteries for me too. Bonaventure was also instrumental in procuring the election of Pope Gregory X – although that Papal election, taking three years, was the longest in history! Gregory rewarded Bonaventure with the titles Cardinal and Bishop of Albano, though it is widely understood when the Papal legate came with the news, Bonaventure smiled and continued to do the washing up.

I thank each person named in this book for being part of my memory these past twenty-five years – for better for worse, for richer for poorer... till death do us part.

My indebted thanks go to my dear friend Noel Botham for his tireless patience and perseverance in making this book see the light of day; to my good friend and publisher John Blake – also for the joy and honour of baptizing two of his grandchildren; to John Wordsworth, editor at Blake-Metro, who has clearly lived up to the name of his distinguished ancestor, William; William Coggan and Benjamin Harnwell for their constant encouragement. For his unstinting kindness in so many ways, Peter Stringfellow – in the angelic basilica that bears his name – offering refuge to distressed sinners and saints alike.

I am also indebted to the late Archbishop Bruno Heim first Apostolic Nuncio to the United Kingdom, for all his remembrances of the late Cardinal Hume. Apart from Bruno Heim and Cardinal Hume himself, Miles Norfolk also provided me with many details of the early years of Hume's reign, as did my good friend Father Norman Brown, who was at Westminster Cathedral for thirty-eight years and was Hume's very close confidante, and a close friend Peter Bander van Duren, a publisher and world authority on heraldry and honours, who was a close friend of Heim and the Cardinal. For their confirmation of events contained within, of which they could provide personal recollections, I am much indebted.

I would also like to congratulate the distinguished political biographer, Anthony Howard, for his prolific work, *Basil Hume: the Monk Cardinal* which deeply explores the Cardinal's political views with regard to the State and human rights. Sadly my own meagre offerings concentrate on his more human and humorous characteristics.

Finally, to those not named here: I still have a lot of memory left – rather like an elephant – plus a very big heart.

Michael Seed
15th July 2009
Feast of St Bonaventure

NOBODY'S CHILD
Michael Seed
with Noel Botham

Michael Seed should have received what every child deserves: love, care and attention, and the chance to be just what he was – an innocent young boy. Instead, from as far back as he can remember, Michael's childhood was nothing but a daily ordeal. His fight for survival against a brutal and emotionally deranged father threatened to destroy his childish innocence and break his potent young spirit.

Yet despite his appalling start in life Michael refused to surrender, and with incredible resilience and determination grew up to become hugely successful and influential in both the church and the secular world.

After a lifetime of silence, he now feels able to tell a story that, although shockingly painful, is a blazing testament to one human's raw courage, and his remarkable ability to finally triumph over the horrors of stolen childhood.

'Painful and profoundly disturbing'
Daily Mail

'If you read any book this year, read this one. He overcame the horrors of his childhood and went on to help others. Believe this story, weep, then cheer in his triumph.'
Martina Cole

This book has the rare ability to distress, shock, inspire and, in Fr Michael's own inimitable way, to amuse its readers as well.'
Independent Catholic News

ISBN 978-1-84454-588-9   £7.99   PB

Metro Publishing Ltd

OUT NOW

TO ORDER SIMPLY CALL THIS NUMBER
+ 44 (0) 207 381 0666

Or visit our website www.johnblakepublishing.co.uk

Free P+P and UK Delivery
(Abroad £3.00 per book)

Prices and availability subject to change without notice